THE ULTIMATE
STUDENT
COOKBOOK
FROM CHICKEN TO CHILI

TIFFANY GOODALL

photography by Claire Peters

FIREFLY BOOKS

CONTENTS

BASIC KITCHEN EQUIPMENT

There are so many gadgets and silly machines that try to make basic tasks easier with their ridiculous mechanisms. I am not a fan of squeezy pipettes and general fad gadgets. Just invest in a few great basics.

Saucepans A small saucepan is great for boiling vegetables, eggs and potatoes. A larger one is useful if you are going to cook a soup or a huge stew for a large group. I have a huge one, which is ideal for a large bolognese.

Measuring Cup Very cheap yet invaluable, a large plastic measuring cup is not only useful for measuring liquids such as water and stock, but can also be used as an impromptu mixing bowl.

Skillet I love a good nonstick skillet for everything from a good breakfast to frying mushrooms—it's an essential item and a solid investment. You can buy a thin-edged skillet that is perfect for crêpes and omelets.

Colander Great for draining water from pasta, rice, potatoes and vegetables. The list is endless. Plastic and metal versions work equally well.

Wok For the best price and quality, my tip is to go to an Asian supermarket to buy your wok. They come in handy all the time, from a quick stir-fry to a gorgeous curry. Don't worry if you haven't got a wok, though: a large high-sided skillet is a perfectly good substitute.

Strainer I tried to live without a strainer as most flours now say "no need to sift." However, I found myself needing one all the time for all sorts of things, especially when baking, so it's a useful thing to have.

Mixing Bowl I would strongly advise a Pyrex mixing bowl, as it's heatproof. Use it for melting chocolate, cake mixing, making pesto, homemade burgers and whipping up swift salad dressings.

Handheld Blender I always use a handheld blender. None of the recipes in this book require a food processor. I use this handheld blender for everything from soups to smoothies and cocktails.

Cutting board I am obsessed with thick wooden cutting boards. Some are quite pricey, but if you are savvy you can find them for good prices—just shop around. Plastic works fine too, however.

Potato Masher Great for mashing not only potatoes, but also vegetables such as butternut squash and carrots.

Vegetable Peeler Essential, especially for a roast lunch.

Can Opener Imperative for the kitchen—from cans of beans to tuna, coconut milk and wonderful canned tomatoes.

Grater Brilliant for grating cheese but also great for grating garlic and ginger.

Whisk Even though you can whisk eggs fairly well with a fork, a whisk is very handy when making omelets as it gives them a lovely light texture. More obviously, you'll need a whisk to whip cream or egg whites.

Spatula A plastic spatula is a great implement for scraping up all the leftovers from a mixing bowl. It's also ideal when you need to fold a mixture gently—as with a chocolate mousse. A metal version is useful when you need to lift and drain fried food, such as when cooking breakfast.

Wooden Spoon or Spatula These are used extensively in baking. They aren't used as much in savory cooking as they tend to absorb the flavors and smells of foods such as garlic, onions and chilies. However, they won't scratch the bottom of nonstick saucepans, unlike metal spoons.

Small Fruit Knife One of these makes cutting or slicing fruit or fine vegetables very easy. It's great to have one when making a delicious fruit salad.

Large Knife My large knife is the most useful of my kitchen tools. I use it to chop herbs, meat, garlic—the works.

PANTRY INGREDIENTS

It's in here somewhere.

When you are living with family it's easy to take the ingredients that fill up the cupboards completely for granted. However, when you arrive at your university halls of residence in your first year, or your appartment or house in subsequent years, there is one thing that is blatantly obvious—the emptiness of the kitchen. The bare shelves and the vacant space in the pantry. It's a killer. However, there are a few basic items that you can buy which will keep for ages and serve you well.

All-Purpose Flour Ideal for everyday baking and for thickening sauces and gravy.

Basmati Rice So good with a curry, or to make a lovely fried rice with various items in your refrigerator.

Canned Tomatoes An absolute necessity for any student kitchen, they are used in bolognese, soups, shepherd's pie …

Chicken/Vegetable Stock Cubes A true must have. Used in gravy, soup, risottos—the list is endless. Chicken will be the most useful, but a beef stock cube is also good for hearty red meat casseroles and stews.

Coconut Milk Amazing to have so you can whip up a Thai green curry, or coconut soup with chicken or shrimp.

English Mustard Perfect for salad dressings, amazing with mashed potato and as an accompaniment with sausages, burgers, etc.

Garlic Garlic will keep in the pantry for 2 to 3 weeks. It can be thrown into all sorts of dishes, from a pasta sauce to a delicious roast chicken. Crushed garlic is seriously potent and a little goes a long way. However, whole garlic cloves can be thrown into a one-pot chicken bake or roast potatoes and they gently exude their flavor.

Ginger Root This adds a fragrant Thai/Asian feel to dishes. It's delicious in a chicken and coconut curry (see page 120) or a beef noodle stir-fry (see page 69). It's fairly pricey but a big piece goes a long way.

Noodles I love egg and rice noodles, which are great for stir-fries.

Olive Oil Great for a lovely dressing or pesto, it is the most used item in my pantry.

YOU WILL NEED:

All-Purpose Flour
Basmati Rice
Canned Tomatoes
Chicken/Vegetable Stock Cubes
Coconut Milk
Dijon Mustard
Garlic
Ginger Root
Noodles
Olive Oil
Onions
Pasta
Ready-Made Pizza Bases
Sunflower Oil
Superfine Sugar
White Wine Vinegar

Onions A must must-have. Buy both red and white varieties; they have a shelf life of 2 to 3 weeks and should be kept in a dry place so they don't begin to rot.

Pasta A student favorite, pasta makes such a delicious, fast dinner.

Ready-Made Pizza Bases Homemade pizzas are epic, and such a laugh to make with your friends.

Sunflower Oil Great for frying, especially breakfast essentials such as sausages or bacon.

Superfine Sugar Used extensively in baking and desserts.

White Wine Vinegar A must-have for salad dressings.

FOOD HYGIENE

Cooking must be fun, as I always say, but you don't want to poison yourself or your friends in the process. Therefore there are a few golden rules.

1 Make sure you have clean hands all the time when you are cooking and wash them after handling raw fish, meat and especially chicken.

2 When handling raw chicken, wash all the equipment that has touched the raw chicken very well. Raw chicken contains very harmful bacteria.

3 When checking to see if chicken is cooked, make sure there are no signs of red and pink and be sure all juices run away totally clear from the meat. Follow all cooking times thoroughly.

4 When reheating a chicken dish, make sure that it is piping hot before you serve it.

5 Be sure to reheat leftover shrimp thoroughly.

6 Make sure that any food stored in the refrigerator is tightly covered with plastic wrap or foil.

7 If you have leftover rice, be sure to reheat it thoroughly. Rice that has been left to cool at room temperature for a long time can contain bacteria.

8 Do not put a hot dish into a cold refrigerator or freezer as this will cause the temperature of the refrigerator or freezer to rise. Let it cool down first, then put it in.

9 Make sure a frozen dish is defrosted totally before cooking it again.

1

BREAKFAST WITH TIFFANY

Breakfasts are famously the most important meal of the day—a fact I've found to be especially true while at university. If I start the day with a fresh healthy breakfast, such as a fresh fruit smoothie or fruit salad, I usually feel more like eating healthily as the day goes on too. There are times, however, when only a serious fried breakfast will do. The traditional Saturday morning fried breakfast after a heavy Friday night is a must, and I know that my roommates all love the smell of frying bacon. It's amazing how many people discover an appetite at the mention of the words "fried breakfast." And don't underestimate the power of what a good egg can do either. I'm a huge fan and, conveniently, they are also an excellent hangover cure …

BREAKFAST SMOOTHIE SERVES 1

Smoothies are so great for breakfast, and with the recipes here feel free to add any soft fruit you like. Berries work wonderfully, as do bananas, raisins, dried fruit, yogurts and milk, so go for it and play around.

YOU WILL NEED:

1 banana, sliced
2 tbsp (30 ml) blueberries
1 tbsp (15 ml) raspberries or
  strawberries
2 tbsp (30 ml) oats or muesli
2½ cups (600 ml) milk

2 Zap it all until all the fruit is crushed and combined with the milk, which usually takes just under 1 minute.

3 Pour into a large glass and enjoy.

1 Put all the ingredients into a pitcher where you can mix them together using a hand-held blender.

Leftovers: Drink it straightaway as it won't keep for long—your delicious smoothie will soon turn from light pink to nasty brown.

ENERGY SMOOTHIE SERVES 1

This is packed full of energy, as bananas are such a great source of protein. Have this for breakfast and you'll be buzzing all morning.

YOU WILL NEED:

1 banana, sliced
1¾ cups (400 ml) milk
3 tbsp (45 ml) plain yogurt,
  although you could also
  use flavored fruit yogurt

1 Place all your ingredients into a pitcher where you can mix them together with a handheld blender.

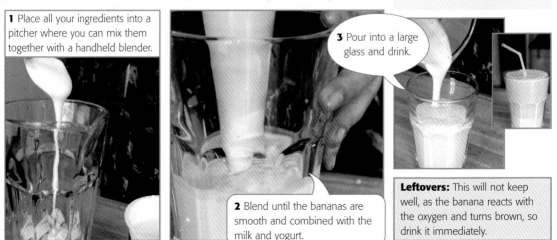

3 Pour into a large glass and drink.

2 Blend until the bananas are smooth and combined with the milk and yogurt.

Leftovers: This will not keep well, as the banana reacts with the oxygen and turns brown, so drink it immediately.

APRICOT SMOOTHIE SERVES 1

Dried fruit is great for your student pantry and it lasts longer and is slightly more economical than fresh fruit. It's also readily available at all times. My favorites are dried apricots and I love them like this.

YOU WILL NEED:
²⁄₃ cup (110 g) dried apricots
1 tbsp (15 ml) raisins
1 banana
2½ cups (600 ml) milk

1 Place the ingredients in a pitcher and use a handheld blender to mix until everything is combined.

2 Pour into a large glass and drink.

Optional Extras: A tsp (5 ml) of honey is delicious in this if you have some lying around. Fresh mint is also amazing and turns it into a very zingy summer drink. **Serving Suggestions:** Tip some ice cubes into your glass and drink it chilled.

BLUEBERRY YOGURT SMOOTHIE SERVES 1

The color of this is amazing and it's so tasty.

YOU WILL NEED:
3 tbsp (45 ml) blueberries
3 tbsp (45 ml) plain or fruit yogurt; my favorite is peach
1¾ cups (400 ml) milk

Amazing.

1 Blend all the ingredients in a pitcher using a handheld blender.

2 Tip the smoothie into a glass.

Optional Extras: Mix in a delicious handful of mixed nuts if you happen to have any.

THE PERFECT POACHED EGG

SERVES 1

The ultimate poached egg is perfectly runny and soft on the inside—total food heaven. And they're not just for breakfast either. Try one on a salad for a delicious, healthy lunch. Everyone has their own little trick to make poached eggs—I think the key is to use a very fresh egg.

YOU WILL NEED:

2 medium eggs

1 slice of bread

1 tsp (5 ml) butter

Bring a pan of water to a fast, rolling boil.

1 Crack your eggs one by one into the saucepan and then reduce the heat to low. Simmer for 4 minutes.

2 Meanwhile, put your bread into the toaster and butter it when done.

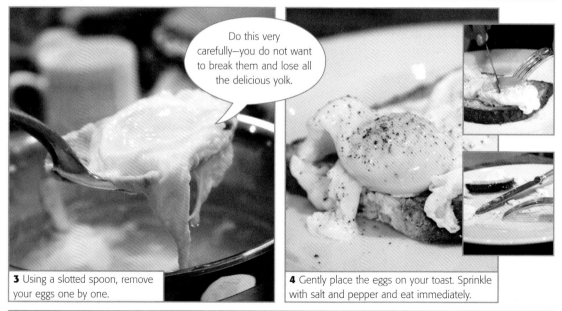

Do this very carefully—you do not want to break them and lose all the delicious yolk.

3 Using a slotted spoon, remove your eggs one by one.

4 Gently place the eggs on your toast. Sprinkle with salt and pepper and eat immediately.

Optional Extras: For pure decadence or for a special occasion, add 1 tbsp (15 ml) of hollandaise sauce over the top and serve with bacon. The official name for this is Eggs Benedict. Chopped chives look great, too.

BOILED EGG AND TOAST
SERVES 1

YOU WILL NEED:
1 medium egg
1 slice of bread
1 tsp (5 ml) butter

I remember when I had my first hangover after a drunken night at a friend's house; it was my mom who (as moms tend to) knew exactly what I needed, and she whipped up two boiled eggs and toast for me in the morning. It was the best meal I've ever had and it hit the spot at the perfect moment. This is a great Sunday night supper too.

Bring a saucepan of water to a boil.

1 Use a spoon to lower the egg into the pan. Boil for 4 to 5 minutes for a runny yolk. For a harder yolk boil for 5 to 6 minutes.

2 Meanwhile, toast your bread, spread it with butter and cut it into strips.

3 Drain your egg and place it on a counter. Hold it in a dish towel as it will be hot. Using a serrated knife, gently cut off the top of the egg and place the rest in an egg cup.

A bread knife is perfect.

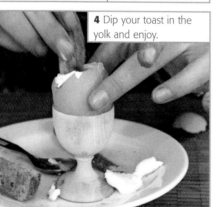

4 Dip your toast in the yolk and enjoy.

Serving Suggestion: You could spoon out all the inside of the egg once it's cooked. Mix it in a bowl with 1 tsp (5 ml) of butter and some salt and pepper, then dip your toast in that. Delicious.

Leftovers: A boiled egg will not stay runny and soft for long, but if you are hard-cooking them, you can keep them in the refrigerator, covered in cold water, for up to 2 days. It takes about 8 minutes to hard-cook an egg. Use them for egg salad sandwiches (see page 49). Great for taking into university for lunch. Just peel the shell off the egg, grate the egg into a bowl, add some mayonnaise, salt and pepper, and put into a sandwich with some lettuce.

SCRAMBLED EGGS ON TOAST

SERVES 1

Scrambled eggs are a cheap and simple meal. I often have them for dinner with some chopped up ham stirred in. If I'm being decadent I have some smoked salmon with them—that's pretty rare though.

YOU WILL NEED:

2 medium eggs
2 tbsp (30 ml) milk
1 tbsp (15 ml) butter
1 tsp (5 ml) vegetable oil
slice of bread

1 Beat the eggs and add the milk, mix well and season with some salt and pepper.

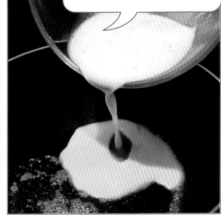

2 Melt the butter in a pan over medium heat. Pour in the egg and milk mixture and turn the heat down to low-medium.

3 Keep stirring the eggs all the time. As the mixture heats up, it'll start to scramble. Stir well to stop the lumps becoming too big.

Perfect breakfast.

4 Toast the bread and tip the scrambled eggs on top. Season with pepper.

Optional Extras: For a serious treat, smoked salmon is the ultimate partner to scrambled eggs.
Serving Suggestions: For me it's perfect on toast with a simple squirt of ketchup.
Leftovers: Not great kept in the refrigerator, so eat up.

FRENCH TOAST WITH MAPLE SYRUP

SERVES 1

This is what I feasted on during my childhood—these days it's a favorite on Sundays. The French call it *pain perdu*: bread soaked in milk and served fried with maple syrup or honey. Works great with day-old bread.

YOU WILL NEED:

1¼ cups (300 ml) milk

2 medium eggs, beaten

2 slices of bread

1 tbsp (15 ml) butter

1 tbsp (15 ml) maple syrup or runny honey

1 Mix the milk and beaten eggs together in a shallow dish.

2 Dip the bread in the mixture, slice by slice, and let soak for a minute to absorb the milk and egg. By the time you have done both slices most of the mixture should have been absorbed.

3 Melt the butter in a skillet set over high heat. Once the butter has melted reduce the heat to medium.

4 Add the bread and fry it for 3 to 4 minutes on each side until golden brown.

Delish …

5 Serve hot drizzled with some maple syrup or runny honey.

Optional Extras: I often use a drop of vanilla extract in the egg and milk mixture; however, it is quite expensive, but if you want to and can afford it, it's great to have in the pantry.

Serving Suggestions: As mentioned above, this is delicious with lots of maple syrup and honey, but it's also almost imperative to have a slice or two of bacon, which can be fried in the same pan used for cooking the bread.

Leftovers: Not great to keep in the refrigerator, so if you have leftovers just go for it and eat them.

JIM'S FRIED BREAKFAST

SERVES 1

YOU WILL NEED:

1 tbsp (15 ml) vegetable oil
2 sausages
2 slices of bacon
3 oz (75 g) mushrooms, sliced
1 tomato, halved
pinch of sugar
1 tsp (5 ml) butter
1 egg
slice of bread

My old friend Jim and I met when we were 17. He always begged for a fried breakfast after a night out; I went on to realize this was a standard request after a night out. A fried breakfast is one of the toughest meals to create perfectly, but the secret is a warm oven. It's the timing that can get you in a tizzy, but if one thing is ready before the rest, just put it in the oven to keep warm while the rest cooks.

Preheat the oven to 275°F (140°C).

1 Pour the oil into a skillet and when it's hot and smoking, add the sausages. Fry them for 7 to 8 minutes, turning occasionally.

2 Add the bacon and cook for another 2 minutes.

3 Next add the mushrooms and tomato halves, flesh side down.

4 Keep turning the sausages, bacon and mushrooms.

5 Flip the tomatoes and season them with a pinch of sugar, and some salt and pepper.

6 After 5 to 6 minutes the mushrooms should be nice and golden, and the meat cooked. The tomatoes will be soft and cooked right through.

After 2 to 3 minutes the egg should become white around the edges.

7 Transfer everything to a plate and put it in the oven to keep warm while you fry the eggs.

8 Melt the butter in the skillet, then tip in the egg. Do this gently so you keep the yolk whole.

9 Sprinkle with a little salt and pepper and, 1 minute later, use a spatula to lift it out of the skillet.

10 Toast the bread and serve with the rest of the food.

Optional Extras: Black or white blood sausage: fry these for 2 to 3 minutes in the same pan as the sausages if you're keen. A poached egg (see page 12), a scrambled egg (see page 14) or even a boiled egg (see page 13) can take the place of the fried egg. Fried bread is bread fried in oil and could be tasty. Also if you have any mashed potatoes lying around, that can taste good fried and served as part of a big brunch.

Serving Suggestions: Serve with a slice of toast and a good cup of coffee or tea.

Leftovers: If you have leftover sausages you can warm them up in a pan or in the oven for 10 minutes. Eat them with mashed potato, or in a sandwich or just cold as a snack for lunch. Leftover sausages and bacon will keep in the refrigerator for 3 days. Fried mushrooms will also keep in the refrigerator for 2 to 3 days and can be warmed up in a saucepan on low heat and served with pasta or alongside a chicken dish.

FRESH FRUIT SALAD
SERVES 5

YOU WILL NEED:
- 1 ripe melon, quartered, peeled, seeded and cut into chunks
- 1 pineapple, cut into chunks, or use the canned version
- 2 kiwis, peeled and chopped
- 2 apples, peeled, cored and chopped
- 2 pears, peeled, seeded and chopped
- 2 tbsp (30 ml) blueberries
- 2 tbsp (30 ml) raspberries
- ¾ cup (175 ml) orange juice

In considerable contrast to a fried breakfast, this is nutritious and so easy to put together with really any fruit you might have lying around. If you make a big fruit salad at the start of the week, and keep it covered in the refrigerator, it's perfect to eat for breakfast or even after dinner. It could also be great taken to university as a snack. It's totally up to you what fruit you use, but make sure that most of it is ripe otherwise it will not taste as good and will be tough to peel and chop. Be aware, however, that bananas tend to go brown and mushy.

1 Combine the melon and pineapple, kiwi, apples and pears in a large bowl.

2 Carefully add the blueberries and raspberries.

4 Mix carefully and keep in the refrigerator until needed.

3 Pour in the orange juice.

Optional Extras: If there's any fruit you want to add or take out then go for it. The orange juice keeps it fresh. A couple of mint leaves and a sprinkle of sugar could always be added.

Serving Suggestions: For breakfast I love fruit salad on some yogurt or even on cereal. As a dessert it's sensational and very light, perfect with some vanilla ice cream or even some softly whipped cream, and you could even stir through some chopped mint too.

Leftovers: This will keep in the refrigerator for 4 to 5 days if tightly covered, although it depends on what fruit you use; for example, bananas do not keep for long at all.

OATMEAL CRAZY
SERVES 1

YOU WILL NEED:
- 1½ cups (350 ml) milk
- ¾ cup (60 g) rolled oats
- 1 tbsp (15 ml) honey

I am officially oatmeal crazy and it's so, so good for you. It's probably the breakfast I have the most, as it's easy and keeps me full all day. Lots of my friends at university have it for breakfast too and it's great either on its own or with a spoonful of honey.

1 Pour the milk into a saucepan and add the oats.

2 As the milk starts bubbling after a few minutes, keep stirring and the oats should expand and start absorbing the milk.

3 It should be ready after 5 to 6 minutes. If it's too thick add some more milk and if it's too runny add more oats and cook for a few minutes longer.

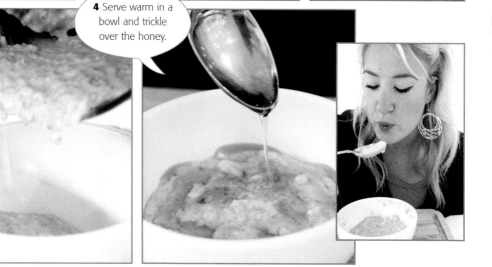

4 Serve warm in a bowl and trickle over the honey.

Optional Extras: You could add a handful of raisins at the beginning, or 1 tbsp (15 ml) of sugar for added sweetness; however, the honey is very sweet. Corn syrup would also be delicious instead of honey.

Serving Suggestions: Lovely with some fresh fruit and some brown sugar sprinkled on top. Lots of people like their oatmeal with a spoonful of strawberry jam stirred in.

Leftovers: Not so great when reheated, so try and eat it all.

HOW TO COOK CRÊPES MAKES 4

I get so excited and love the whole experience of making crêpes. It's high time we made more of them! They are ideal for breakfast— quick to make and guaranteed to give you lots of energy for the day ahead. Make a good batter, let it rest, make sure you use a good nonstick skillet with lots of delicious fillings ready and then offer some to your roommates, if you're feeling generous.

YOU WILL NEED:
scant 1½ cups (200 g) all-purpose flour
2 large eggs
2½ cups (600 ml) milk
½ tbsp (7 ml) sugar (for sweet crêpes) or ½ tsp (2 ml) salt (for savory crêpes)
scant ½ cup (100 g) butter (2 tbsp/30 ml butter per crêpe)

If you have a handheld blender you can use it to make the batter extra smooth.

1 Sift the all-purpose flour in a large mixing bowl and make a well in the center of the flour. Break the eggs into the well then add the milk.

2 Whisk well, making sure there are no lumps.

3 Add ½ tsp (2 ml) of salt if you are making savory crêpes or ½ tbsp (7 ml) of sugar if you're making sweet crêpes. If you want your batter to make both types, just leave any salt or sugar out of it completely.

4 Melt 4 tbsp (50 ml) butter in a nonstick skillet over medium heat. Add a ladleful of batter.

You can use a spatula if you're feeling nervous

5 Swirl the batter to the edges of the pan and then return it to the heat for 1 minute to cook.

6 Flip the crêpe over and then cook for 1 minute more.

7 Tip onto a plate and add the filling of your choice. Repeat with the rest of the crêpe batter. If you're making a lot keep them separated by sheets of waxed paper and keep warm in the oven at its lowest setting.

Optional Extras: If you're making a batch of savory crêpes, add some chopped herbs to the batter to brighten it up.
Serving Suggestions: Fill with a whole variety of fillings, such as ham and cheese, cheese and mushrooms, lemon and sugar, chocolate and banana, banana and ice cream … .
Leftovers: You can make the batter and keep it covered in the refrigerator for 2 days, but it's best used on the same day.

HAM AND CHEESE CRÊPES MAKES 4

These crêpes remind me of trips to France—the French cook them to perfection.

YOU WILL NEED:
scant 1½ cups (200 g) all-purpose flour
2 large eggs
2½ cups (600 ml) milk
½ tsp (2 ml) salt
scant ½ cup (100 g) butter
12 oz (350 g) ham, sliced
4 oz (110 g) cheddar cheese, grated

1 Make your crêpe batter (see opposite).

2 Melt 4 tbsp (50 ml) butter in a nonstick skillet over medium heat. Add a ladleful of batter.

3 Swirl the mixture evenly around the pan.

4 Sprinkle in some cheese and ham

5 After a minute, use a spatula to flip the crêpe in half, and cook for another minute.

The cheese will become really gooey and gorgeous.

Tip onto a plate and eat immediately.

Optional Extras: You could add some tomato and a few herbs, such as parsley or cilantro, at the same time as the ham and cheese. Mushrooms would also be great. Fry them for 2 to 3 minutes before adding them to the crêpe.
Serving Suggestions: If you're in a hurry, wrap it in foil for a breakfast on the move.
Leftovers: Don't try to keep any cooked crêpes in the refrigerator as they'll become soggy. If you have leftover batter just keep it covered in the refrigerator for up to 2 days.

BASIC SWEET CRÊPES MAKES 4

These are sweet, but not too sweet, allowing you to have lots and lots of them. Delicious.

YOU WILL NEED:
scant 1½ cups (200 g) all-purpose flour
2 large eggs
2½ cups (600 ml) milk
4½ tbsp (68 ml) sugar
scant ½ cup (100 g) butter
juice of 2 lemons

1 Make your crêpes (see page 20).

2 Tip your crêpes onto a plate.

3 Squeeze lemon juice over each crêpe and then sprinkle with 1 tbsp (15 ml) of sugar.

Ouch!

4 Roll up each crêpe and enjoy.

Optional Extras: A drizzle of honey could be so delicious here, or a spoonful of plain yogurt.
Serving Suggestions: Perfect just as they are.
Leftovers: Keep the batter in the refrigerator, covered, for up to 2 days.

DECADENT CHOCOLATE AND BANANA CRÊPES MAKES 4

YOU WILL NEED:
scant 1½ cups (200 g)
all-purpose flour
2 large eggs
2½ cups (600 ml) milk
½ tbsp (7 ml) sugar
scant ½ cup (100 g) butter
4 oz (110 g) chocolate spread
2 bananas, sliced

The combination of chocolate and banana in a hot crêpe is unbeatable. Perfect to get everyone in the party mood. In the summer throw in a few red berries and it's a whole new story.

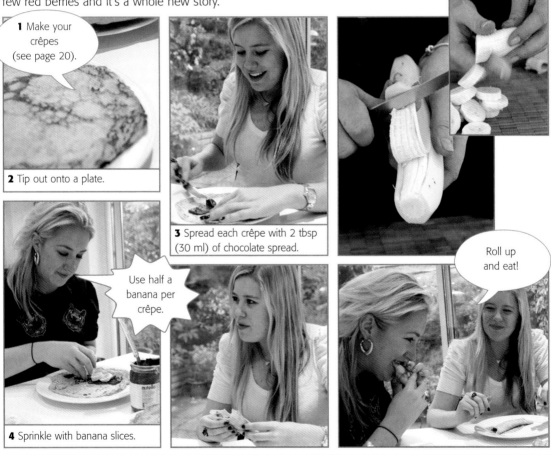

1 Make your crêpes (see page 20).

2 Tip out onto a plate.

3 Spread each crêpe with 2 tbsp (30 ml) of chocolate spread.

Use half a banana per crêpe.

4 Sprinkle with banana slices.

Roll up and eat!

Optional Extras: Some chopped fresh mint would be gorgeous here, as would some mini marshmallows, raspberries or strawberries.
Serving Suggestions: I am a huge fan of chocolate and strawberries or raspberries, so I'd quite like a few of those in my crêpe, too.
Leftovers: Keep any leftover batter, covered, in the refrigerator for up to 2 days.

2

REAL
FAST
FOOD

Life at university is fast and furious. Whether facing a long day of lectures, or rushing to get out of the house for a night out, time is always of the essence. This is where this chapter can help, as it shows how to throw a few basics together for maximum results. All the recipes serve one, perfect for weeknight suppers when everyone is busy doing their own thing. Pasta is a reliably great option, and it's always tasty. I've included a few omelet ideas too, as they're so quick, cheap and versatile. Just throw in whatever you have—ham, tomato, cheese … Another economical yet delicious option, risotto, is perfect for midweek suppers. Plus it has the bonus, as you stir away, of leaving you with one hand free for a drink.

HOW TO COOK PASTA

SERVES 1

YOU WILL NEED:

4 cups (1 liter) boiling water

pinch of salt

½ tsp (2 ml) olive oil

5 oz (150 g) dried pasta, such as spaghetti, penne or pasta shells

Pasta is a key ingredient in the kitchen at university, partly because it's ideal hangover food. An ultra delicious pasta dish can be put together in a very short space of time—just what you need after a long day. It's cheap to buy and dried pasta can be kept in your student pantry for a long time. However, like so much in life, it can be the simplest things that can be hardest to get right. So here are a few tips and ideas that I find helpful whenever I'm cooking pasta.

Pasta is cooked in a big pan of salted boiling water with the lid off. A drop of olive oil helps the pasta to stay loose and not stick together. Dried pasta is cooked for around 9 to 12 minutes; the package will show the ideal time for the type you've bought. Fresh pasta cooks much faster, usually 2 to 4 minutes. Dried pasta is cheaper and keeps for longer though, so is usually better for student kitchens. One more thing to remember: hot pasta waits for no one, so eat it immediately.

1 Bring the water to a boil and add the salt and the olive oil.

2 Add the pasta and stir once to stop it sticking together.

3 The pasta will usually take between 9 and 12 minutes to cook, depending on its size and shape. The package will tell you how long to cook it, but test it before you drain it by giving it a taste. It will be ready when it's soft, however I like mine when it still has a bit of bite to it.

4 Drain the pasta in a colander and serve it with a sauce of your choice. How quick and easy!

TOMATO AND GARLIC SAUCE

SERVES 1

This is a very basic tasty pasta sauce, but if you want to spice it up there are plenty of options. See my list of optional extras, below, for a few ideas of what you could put in the sauce to make it even more delicious.

YOU WILL NEED:

9 oz (250 g) canned chopped tomatoes

½ red chili, seeded and chopped

2 garlic cloves, peeled and crushed

½ tsp (2 ml) sugar

1 Begin cooking your pasta (see opposite).

4 Drain your cooked pasta and stir it into the sauce.

2 Put all the sauce ingredients in a pan over medium heat.

3 When the sauce is bubbling slowly, season it with salt and pepper.

This dish couldn't be quicker and the chili gives it a cheeky kick. A bit of grated cheese and black pepper on top would finish it off perfectly.

Optional Extras: Try adding any or all of the following to the basic tomato and garlic sauce: bacon bits, mushrooms, finely chopped red bell peppers, chopped basil, chopped parsley, 1 tbsp (15 ml) white or red wine.

Serving Suggestions: Delicious on pasta with some grated cheese or with some fresh basil and a green salad.

Leftovers: This sauce will freeze very well, and will keep in the refrigerator for 2 to 3 days. If you have any leftovers, spoon them onto some pita bread, a slice of ciabatta or toast with some cheese and ham and you have a sort of mini pizza. It would also be a great base for tomato soup; just add around 2 cups (500 ml) of vegetable or chicken stock.

MAGIC MUSHROOM SAUCE SERVES 1

This is so simple yet full of flavor. I use crème fraîche as it's a healthy alternative to cream, but if you have some cream you can easily use that instead. It's perfect with pasta and you can whip this up while your pasta is boiling. In 10 minutes you have a filling supper.

YOU WILL NEED:

⅓ cup (75 g) butter
1 scallion, chopped
1 garlic clove, peeled and crushed
3 oz (75 g) mushrooms, sliced
1 tbsp (15 ml) olive oil (optional)
1–2 tbsp (15–30 ml) crème fraîche
1 lemon, quartered
handful of chopped chives

1 Cook your pasta (see page 26).

2 Melt the butter in a pan set over low heat. Add the scallion and garlic and cook for 5 minutes until they are soft.

3 Raise the heat and add the mushrooms. If they start to look a little dry add a splash of olive oil. When the mushrooms have become soft, add some salt and pepper.

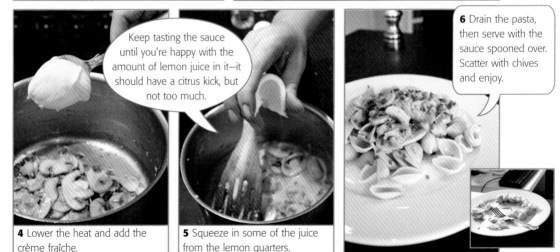

Keep tasting the sauce until you're happy with the amount of lemon juice in it—it should have a citrus kick, but not too much.

6 Drain the pasta, then serve with the sauce spooned over. Scatter with chives and enjoy.

4 Lower the heat and add the crème fraîche.

5 Squeeze in some of the juice from the lemon quarters.

Optional Extras: Herbs with this are delicious, so if you have any lying around add them. My first choice would be some chopped chives or cilantro.

Leftovers: Any leftover sauce can be kept in the refrigerator until the next day; I wouldn't recommend any longer as the recipe contains dairy products and these go bad quickly. Instead of eating it with pasta again, it would be delicious gently reheated and served on toast or a bagel. Alternatively, serve the leftover sauce in a baked potato—true comfort food.

MA'S CARBONARA SAUCE **SERVES 1**

My mom makes the most delicious carbonara sauce—creamy, garlicky and truly delicious! The ingredients are basic: eggs, cream and milk are items I often find lying around in my refrigerator.

1 Cook your pasta (see page 26).

YOU WILL NEED:

1 tbsp (15 ml) olive oil
2 garlic cloves, peeled and crushed
3½ oz (100 g) unsmoked or normal bacon, chopped roughly
1 medium egg, whisked
2 tbsp (30 ml) grated cheddar cheese
½ cup (125 ml) heavy cream
1 tbsp (15 ml) milk

Set your dirty skillet aside for later.

3 Tip the bacon onto a piece of paper towel to drain.

2 Heat the olive oil in a large skillet, and add the garlic and bacon. Cook over medium heat for 5 minutes until the bacon is brown, stirring regularly.

4 Mix up the egg, bacon, cheese, cream and milk, and season with salt and pepper. Stir well.

5 Check your pasta and when it's ready, drain it and tip it into the large skillet you used earlier. Add the egg mixture and gently heat it for 1 minute over low-medium heat. This is very important because if the heat is too high you will end up with scrambled eggs!

6 Taste to check the seasoning and then serve.

Optional Extras: Italian parsley would be tasty, chopped and scattered over the top.
Serving Suggestion: A very simple green salad is great with this, as it can be quite rich and the lettuce just mellows it all.
Leftovers: If you have any leftover sauce, it can be kept it in the refrigerator until the following day. Reheat it slowly in a pan, adding 1 tsp (5 ml) of cream to make it a little less dry.

BASIL, GARLIC, FETA, ARUGULA AND OLIVE OIL SPAGHETTI SERVES 1

YOU WILL NEED:

3 tbsp (45 ml) olive oil

2 tomatoes, sliced

5 oz (150 g) dried spaghetti

2 garlic cloves, peeled and chopped finely

2 tbsp (30 ml) roughly chopped basil

4 oz (110 g) feta cheese, crumbled

handful of arugula or lettuce leaves

I came up with this once while looking in the refrigerator and stuck for what to have for dinner. Lying around in my typically untidy student refrigerator were some garlic, feta cheese, arugula, tomatoes and some basil, so I put it all together as a sauce with some olive oil, served it with spaghetti and wow, it's now one of my staple and favorite dishes. The handy thing about this dish is you can substitute ingredients for what YOU have in your refrigerator. So if you have some peppers or parsley, throw them in. Similarly cheddar or goat cheese would work well instead of feta.

3 Drain the pasta and tip it back into the pan. Add the garlic and basil mixture.

Preheat the oven to 350°F (180°C).

1 Pour 1 tbsp (15 ml) of the oil over the tomatoes in a baking dish. Put in the oven for 10 minutes.

2 Cook your pasta (see page 26). Meanwhile, put the garlic and basil into a bowl, add the remaining 2 tbsp (30 ml) of olive oil and mix.

4 Remove the tomatoes from the oven.

5 Tip the pasta into a bowl and add the hot tomatoes. Mix well and lots of tomato juice should come out of them.

6 Add the crumbled feta cheese and season with some salt and pepper.

7 Serve scattered with the arugula leaves. Eat immediately.

Optional Extras: There isn't really a limit with something like this. Peppers would be great, any kind of cheese, chives, cilantro, canned tomatoes, chili, bacon … Feel free to go right ahead and add whatever you like.

Serving Suggestions: As you have your salad greens on top, there is no need to mess around with a side salad, just have a glass of wine or a beer and go for it.

Leftovers: This will keep in the refrigerator for a day. Warm it up the following day in a saucepan set over low-medium heat, adding another 1 tbsp (15 ml) of olive oil. I think it's best eaten immediately though, so eat up.

MUSHROOM AND RED ONION RISOTTO

SERVES 1

YOU WILL NEED:

generous 1 cup (250 ml) water
2 vegetable stock cubes
4 tbsp (60 ml) butter
2 garlic cloves, peeled and chopped finely
½ red onion, peeled and chopped finely
⅓ cup (75 g) arborio rice
½ glass of white wine (optional)
3 oz (75 g) mushrooms, sliced
2 tbsp (30 ml) grated Parmesan cheese
handful of arugula leaves

Risotto is one of my real favorite dishes to cook, let alone eat. It takes about 15 to 20 minutes to make and you can let yourself unwind as you monotonously stir your risotto and watch it become creamier and creamier. If you can master a risotto, which is very simple to make, you are onto a real winner. It's great to throw in whatever you like, anything from goat cheese to mushrooms. If you decide to cook some for friends, you'll be surprised how many will be quietly impressed.

1 Boil the water in a pan then crumble in your stock cubes. Reduce the heat to low and keep the stock simmering while you make the risotto.

2 In a skillet, melt the butter over low-medium heat.

3 Add the garlic and the onion. Reduce the heat to low and cook for 5 minutes until the onion is nice and soft.

5 Stir well so the rice soaks up all the delicious melted butter, onion and garlic. Next add the wine, if you're using it.

4 Increase the heat to medium-high and add the rice.

Stir all the time to stop the rice sticking to the bottom of the pan.

8 This process should take 15 to 20 minutes. Keep tasting your risotto until it becomes deliciously creamy but still with a little bite to it.

6 When the wine has been absorbed by the rice add a ladleful of stock and a pinch of salt.

7 Add the mushrooms and stir. Once each ladle of stock has been absorbed, add another.

9 When all the stock has been absorbed, stir in the Parmesan and serve immediately.

Some arugula leaves and grated Parmesan would be ideal as an accompaniment.

Optional Extras: This is a very basic risotto recipe using just mushrooms. However you could also add herbs, such as rosemary, thyme (delicious in this), parsley or even chives. A little bacon tastes amazing in a risotto, too. Really the choice is yours. If you don't want to use a red onion or don't have one then a white onion works just as well. I just love the flavor of red onion in risotto.

Serving Suggestions: Risotto is often quite rich, so a handful of arugula leaves really complements it.

Leftovers: Risotto is best eaten immediately. A great excuse to eat it all! If you do have leftovers, reheat them thoroughly.

GOAT CHEESE AND ROSEMARY RISOTTO

SERVES 1

The flavor combinations in this are absolutely sensational. It's very simple and delicious and really worth trying out. Since goat cheese is not as cheap as, say, cheddar, then maybe do it as a treat, but you could easily substitute cheddar or even some blue cheese. Also, it's amazing where rosemary grows. At university I found it growing in the backyard, so have a look around your backyard or your friends' backyards and you might find some growing near you.

1 Boil the water in a pan then crumble in your stock cubes. Reduce the heat to low and keep the stock simmering while you make the risotto.

3 Reduce the heat to low and add the garlic and the onion.

2 In a saucepan, melt the butter over low-medium heat.

5 Increase the heat to medium-high and add the rice and the rosemary. Stir well so the rice soaks up the butter, onion and garlic. Next add the wine, if you're using it.

4 Cook for 5 minutes until the onion is soft.

7 Stir all the time to stop the rice sticking to the bottom of the pan. When each ladle of stock has been absorbed, add another. This process should take 15 to 20 minutes.

Keep tasting your risotto until it becomes deliciously creamy but still has a bit of bite to it.

6 When the wine has been absorbed by the rice, add a ladleful of stock and a pinch of salt.

8 Crumble in most of the cheese.

9 Season, stir and serve topped with the remaining cheese.

Optional Extras: Some chopped bacon bits would be delicious. A handful of arugula or watercress on top of the cooked risotto when you're ready to serve works well too. A drizzle of balsamic vinegar, if you have any, really brings out all the flavors—just add 1 tsp (5 ml) of this when you're ready to serve.

Serving Suggestions: This risotto is delicious if you mix in some pesto as well (see page 65). The risotto goes deliciously green and is known as a risotto verde.

Leftovers: Eat it all up, as this won't keep.

CAULIFLOWER CHEESE SERVES 1

This is great as a side dish with a roast or meaty dish, but don't underestimate how great it is just on its own as a speedy supper. While the cauliflower is cooking you can whip up a gorgeous, cheesy sauce and then brown it off under a broiler or in the oven—perfect comfort food.

YOU WILL NEED:

½ head cauliflower, broken up into little florets

3 tbsp (45 ml) butter, plus extra for greasing

generous ¼ cup (40 g) flour

¾ cup (175 ml) milk

12 oz (350 g) cheddar cheese, grated

Preheat the oven to 350°F (180°C).

1 Boil a large pan of water and add the cauliflower. Boil for 6 to 7 minutes until the stalks are soft when pressed with a knife, then drain.

2 Meanwhile, gently melt the butter in a saucepan. Add the flour and stir well for 1 to 2 minutes.

3 Add the milk.

4 Stir well with a wooden spoon or a whisk for 4 to 5 minutes.

The lumps should start to dissolve and the milk will become thicker.

5 Stir in three-quarters of the cheese until it dissolves. Remove from the heat.

6 Grease the bottom of an ovenproof dish with butter and then scatter in the cauliflower.

The size I use is 8 inches (20 cm) long, 6 inches (15 cm) wide and 2½ inches (6 cm) deep, but it's not critical to use one exactly this size.

7 Pour over the cheese sauce, then scatter with the remaining grated cheese and bake in the oven for 10 to 15 minutes until bubbling and golden.

How good is that?

Heh heh!

Optional Extras: Add strips of ham over the cooked cauliflower before you add the cheese sauce—a delicious twist.
Serving Suggestions: This is great comfort food; serve with some boiled peas on the side for real home cooking.
Leftovers: Cheese sauce will keep in the refrigerator for up to 2 days. To reheat, pour it into a saucepan and heat up VERY slowly, stirring all the time. You could serve it this time with macaroni as mac and cheese. Cook 9 oz (250 g) macaroni in a pot of boiling water for 8 to 10 minutes, then drain and mix into the hot cheese sauce. Transfer to a baking dish and level the top. Scatter over the remaining cheese and bake for 15 to 20 minutes until golden and bubbling.

HOW TO MAKE A TOASTED SANDWICH

Toasted sandwiches are the best, most wonderful food when you've had a night out. Forget the calories, just add whatever you can find to make a gorgeous, fat hot sandwich. My favorite ingredient in a toasty is cheese. I am assuming that you won't have a toasted sandwich maker. It might seem odd to write a recipe for a toasted sandwich, but I always want ideas for juicy mouthwatering fillings.

HAM AND CHEESE TOAST SERVES 1

YOU WILL NEED:
2 slices of bread
1 tsp (5 ml) butter
1 tsp (5 ml) mayonnaise
3 slices of ham
3 slices of cheddar cheese

1 Place the bread slices in your toaster and toast for 2 minutes until brown.

2 Remove from the toaster and spread with the butter and mayo.

3 Add the slices of ham and cheese.

4 Then sandwich the bread slices together.

Easy peasy.

Optional Extras: You could add some lovely sliced tomatoes or even some lettuce leaves.
Serving Suggestions: Eat with a dollop of ketchup on the side.

BANANA TOAST **SERVES 1**

This might sound like a strange combination, but I used to adore banana toast when I was a little girl—just adored them. I sometimes have them now and again, but it's got to be a great one after the bar. It hits both sweet and savory cravings, killing two birds with one stone.

YOU WILL NEED:
2 slices of bread
1 banana
1 tsp (5 ml) butter
1 tsp (5 ml) sugar

1 Toast your bread.

2 Slice up the banana.

3 Butter the toast and then pile the banana onto one slice.

4 Sprinkle with the sugar and then sandwich them both together.

Optional Extras: You could add 1 tsp (5 ml) of chocolate spread here, which would be amazing. Brown sugar would work very well too.
Serving Suggestions: Eat with a lovely cup of coffee.

THE T CLUB **SERVES 1**

I regularly make this for friends, who've named it the T Club. In my eyes it's the king of the toasted sandwiches. Don't worry if you're missing some of the ingredients, just put in what you have or want.

1 Toast the bread. Meanwhile, get your ingredients ready.

2 Spread the toast with the butter, mayo and sweet pepper sauce.

4 Sandwich the whole lot together with the other slice of toast and carefully cut diagonally in half.

3 Then pile up your cold bacon if you have it and/or the chicken. Place your ham, cheese and avocado slices over the top.

5 Secure each half together using a toothpick.

Optional Extras: Add or remove what you like. Lettuce leaves are lovely in toast. Try adding ½ tsp (2 ml) of pesto (see page 65). You could also turn this into a wrap by placing all the ingredients in a tortilla.
Serving Suggestions: Eat with a load of napkins nearby, as you're guaranteed to spill.
Leftovers: Not worth keeping, so just eat it.

THE ULTIMATE CHEESE ON TOAST SERVES 1

This is my stepmom's recipe for cheese on toast. It is utterly delicious. The onion's flavor mellows under the broiler but still manages to provide a little extra kick. It's classic comfort food.

YOU WILL NEED:

1 tbsp (15 ml) finely chopped onion

5 oz (150 g) cheddar cheese, grated

2 tbsp (30 ml) milk

1 tsp (5 ml) Worcestershire sauce

2 slices of white bread

1 tsp (5 ml) butter

Preheat the broiler to high.

1 In a bowl, mix the onion, cheese, milk and Worcestershire sauce. Season well with salt and pepper.

Serve hot.

2 Spoon the mixture evenly over the bread slices.

3 Place under a hot broiler.

4 Cook for 5 to 7 minutes until golden brown and bubbling.

Optional Extras: You could lay 2 slices of ham on each slice of bread before you spoon on the cheese mixture and then you have the ultimate ham and cheese on toast.
Serving Suggestions: Serve with a good squirt of ketchup and that's it.

HAM AND CHEESE OMELET SERVES 1

YOU WILL NEED:

2 eggs

1 tbsp (15 ml) milk

2 tbsp (30 ml) butter

1 tsp (5 ml) oil

2 tbsp (30 ml) grated
cheddar cheese

2 tbsp (30 ml) chopped ham

Omelets are the *ultimate* fast food; they should be cooked in one minute and on high heat. Follow these basic tips and your omelet should be perfect. Use a nonstick pan, preferably 8–9 inches (20–22 cm) in diameter. I use mainly butter and a drizzle of oil. This is because butter cooked on very high heat burns, but not once you add a little oil.

1 Crack the eggs into a bowl and add the milk. Use a whisk to mix just until the eggs and milk are combined, as you need to keep some air in the eggs to create a fluffy omelet. Add a good pinch of both salt and pepper.

2 Put your pan onto high heat and add the butter and oil. When they are hot, after about 1 minute, add the egg mixture.

3 Using a spatula, start scraping the mixture from the outside of the pan into the middle. Tilt the pan to allow any uncooked liquid egg to flow into the gaps and cook. It should take no more than a minute to cook. Don't forget the heat should be set to HIGH, so you'll need to work quickly.

4 Scatter the cheese and ham over the middle of the omelet and shake the pan around a little. Carefully flip half of the omelet over the other half as this will make the cheese melt faster.

5 After another 10 seconds, tip the folded omelet onto a plate and serve.

Optional Extras: As far as fillings are concerned you can really be as creative and have as much fun creating your favorite omelet as you want. They are great meals to use up leftovers like mushrooms, bacon, tomatoes, boiled potatoes or chicken. Add some chopped tomatoes for a delicious ham, cheese and tomato omelet.
Serving Suggestions: Eat with a green salad for a fresh feel.
Leftovers: This does not keep well or reheat well, but if you're only making one you should manage to eat it all.

SPANISH OMELET

SERVES 1

The Spanish call this a *tortilla de patatas* and serve it either hot or cold. It's ideal sliced up for picnics or a packed lunch. This is a good dish for using up leftovers as well, and you can really put what you want in it. I make mine with potatoes, onions and tomatoes, but feel free to leave out or add ingredients depending on what you have.

YOU WILL NEED:

1 tsp (5 ml) oil
3 small new potatoes, sliced thinly
2 tbsp (30 ml) butter
3 eggs, beaten
1 medium tomato, diced finely
½ onion, peeled and sliced finely

1 Heat the oil in an 8–9-inch (20–22 cm) skillet over high heat. Add the potato slices and a good pinch of salt. Reduce the heat to medium and cook for about 5 minutes until golden. Remove the cooked potatoes from the pan and set aside.

Don't worry about drawing the edges in as you would with a normal omelet—you want the edges to set.

2 Using the same pan, melt the butter over medium heat, then tip in the beaten eggs.

3 Add the cooked potato slices, tomato and onion.

4 After about 3 minutes you should see the omelet begin to set. Next you need to turn the omelet onto the other side so it cooks evenly. To do this find a plate that's bigger than the pan you're using, turn the plate upside down (covering the pan) and turn the omelet onto the plate.

5 Slide the omelet back into the pan to cook the other side for 2 minutes. Serve.

Optional Extras: Be really experimental and add what you like. Bacon, peas, red onions and pepperoni work well.
Serving Suggestions: Just as good cold and perfect to take to the library or university as a snack. Cute as well with some drinks if you have friends coming around. You could cook it in the morning and serve it chopped up as snacks.
Leftovers: This will keep in the refrigerator for up to 2 days.

ONE POT CHICKEN THIGHS SERVES 1

This is great when I get home tired and hungry. So quick and easy—you literally throw everything you want with your chicken into a roasting tray, pop it into the hot oven for 20 minutes and there you go. Easy and delicious. Don't forget you could always replace the chicken thighs with a piece of fish, if you want a change.

YOU WILL NEED:
- 1–2 chicken thighs
- 2 garlic cloves, peeled
- ½ red onion, peeled, halved and sliced
- 1 tomato, cut into wedges
- 2 tbsp (30 ml) olive oil
- large sprig of rosemary
- basil leaves, to serve (optional)

Preheat the oven to 400°F (200°C).

1 Put the chicken thighs, garlic, onion and tomato in a roasting tray.

2 Drizzle with the olive oil and sprinkle with a pinch of salt.

Check that the chicken is cooked properly by cutting it open at the thickest point to make sure there is no sign of pink.

3 Add a sprig of rosemary and roast in the oven for 20 minutes until the chicken is cooked.

4 Tip onto a plate, add some basil, if you have it and serve.

Optional Extras: Try roasting the chicken thighs with some new potatoes, lemon wedges and thyme. A dash of white wine would make it even better.

Serving Suggestions: To make a heartier dish, serve with some mashed potato, chips or roast some baby new potatoes with the chicken.

Leftovers: Any leftover chicken will keep in the refrigerator for up to 2 days and can be used in a salad, pasta or risotto.

CHICKEN WRAPPED IN BACON SERVES 1

This is super speedy and very delicious, not to mention plain simple. The bacon smells amazing while it cooks, so you'll be guaranteed to be really hungry by the time it's ready to eat.

YOU WILL NEED:

1 slice of bacon, smoked or unsmoked

1 chicken breast

1 tbsp (15 ml) olive oil

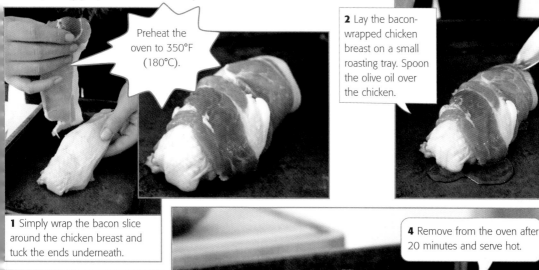

Preheat the oven to 350°F (180°C).

2 Lay the bacon-wrapped chicken breast on a small roasting tray. Spoon the olive oil over the chicken.

1 Simply wrap the bacon slice around the chicken breast and tuck the ends underneath.

4 Remove from the oven after 20 minutes and serve hot.

3 Put in the oven for 20 minutes.

Optional Extras: I have left this very simple to prove how easy it can be. However, you could use garlic and crush it then rub it onto the chicken breast skin before you wrap it in the bacon. You might also want to take a sprig of rosemary or thyme and tuck it under the bacon for added flavor. Another delicious thing to do is take a slice of cheese (cheddar would be fine, but another great option would be a little bit of blue cheese) just place a small slice of it under the bacon before you put it all in the oven.

Serving Suggestions: Serve with a drizzle of olive oil and some pasta, rice or a juicy tomato salad.

Leftovers: You can keep the cooked chicken in your refrigerator for 2 days. To reheat it, put it in an ovenproof dish, cover it with foil and warm it in an oven set to 225°F (110°C). It should take about 15 minutes to become piping hot. Served cold, it would be delicious sliced in a salad or with some couscous. You could even take it to university for lunch.

3

FOOD ON THE MOVE

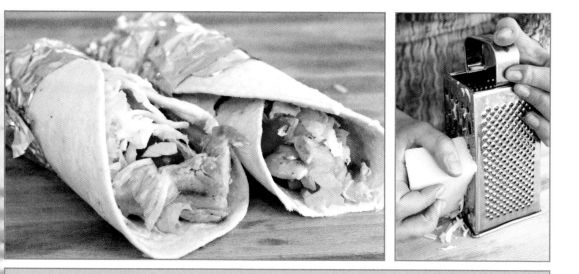

Every student becomes a master at being thrifty with their money. Days are spent hurrying from one lecture or tutorial to the next, and then before you know it, it's lunchtime. Regularly buying a salad or a sandwich and a drink can start to cost a fair bit, but if you make your own food to take into university you can save your money for much better things instead.

I've included my favorite wraps, sandwiches, salads and couscous recipes here. They've served me well, being both delicious and portable. None of them take long to make, just give yourself 10 minutes extra in the morning and you'll be good to go.

TUNA AND SCALLION PITA SERVES 1

Sandwiches are probably the most common item found in a lunch box, and they are great. I love fiddling around with the fillings and even the breads. Normal bread is great, but rolls, wraps and pitas are also very delicious and it's good to keep changing your sandwich so you don't get bored. I always have wraps in my pantry as they are healthy for lunch, and then in the evening transform into fajitas, another firm favorite.

YOU WILL NEED:
7 oz (200 g/1 can) tuna in brine
1 scallion, chopped
1 tbsp (15 ml) mayonnaise
1 tbsp (15 ml) tomato ketchup
1 medium tomato, chopped
1–2 pita breads
2–4 lettuce leaves

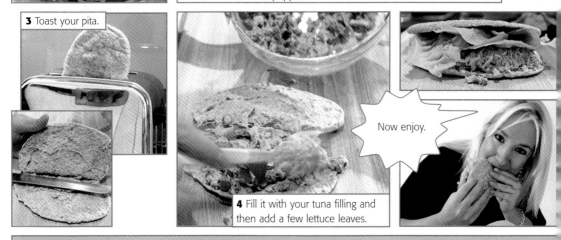

1 Drain the liquid out of your can of tuna. Most cans of tuna are sold in brine, salt water or oil. I always get the one in brine as it's the healthiest and tastiest.

I was on vacation with a friend a few years ago, and when she made her picnic lunches for the beach she always put ketchup in her tuna sandwiches. I thought that was pretty odd at first but tried it and I have never looked back. Amazing ...

2 Mix the tuna, scallion, mayonnaise, ketchup and tomato. Taste and season with salt and pepper.

3 Toast your pita.

Now enjoy.

4 Fill it with your tuna filling and then add a few lettuce leaves.

Optional Extras: Capers, chopped chives.
Serving Suggestions: You could fill your lunch box with delicious treats such as potato chips, a chocolate bar and a mix of chopped carrots, cucumber and celery.
Leftovers: Any extra filling will keep in the refrigerator for 1 to 2 days and would be delicious in a baked potato.

EGG SALAD SANDWICHES SERVES 1

Egg salad reminds me of the delicious sandwiches on white bread I used to have in my lunch boxes when I was little. It's so simple but a true tradition and a staple sandwich filler. Yum.

YOU WILL NEED:
2 medium eggs
1 tbsp (15 ml) mayonnaise
1 tsp (5 ml) butter
2 slices of bread

1 Bring a pan of water to a boil. Lower the eggs, one by one, into the pan using a large spoon.

2 Cook for 8 minutes, then drain and refill the pan with cold water. Let the eggs cool for 2 minutes. When cool, gently knock the eggs on the side. Peel away and discard the shell.

3 I use a grater to grate the cooked eggs into a bowl, but you could also chop or slice the eggs or even mash them with a fork.

4 Stir the mayonnaise into the egg and add lots of salt and pepper.

5 Butter the bread and add the filling.

Optional Extras: Chopped chives, lettuce.
Serving Suggestion: I think this is great with good chunky hunky white bread.
Leftovers: The filling will keep in an airtight container in the refrigerator for 2 days.
Other Sandwich Filling Ideas: Ham and cheese, ham and mustard, chicken and corn, chicken and mayonnaise (also nice in baked potatoes), ham and tomato or classic cucumber.
It's great to beef sandwiches up with some lettuce, cucumber, mayonnaise, and a bit of salt and pepper.

POTATO, BACON AND SCALLION SALAD

SERVES 1

This is simply gorgeous as a lunch and I love it with some chicken or just on its own for a nifty little supper.

1 Bring a pan of water to a boil and carefully add the potatoes. Boil for 10 minutes.

2 Meanwhile, heat the oil in a skillet and add the bacon. Fry on medium heat for 4 to 5 minutes until crispy and golden. Tip onto paper towels to soak up some of the oil.

3 Make sure the potatoes are cooked by pressing one with the tip of a sharp knife. It should be soft enough to go in easily.

4 Drain the potatoes and tip them into a bowl. Add the crispy bacon and scallions and mix in the mayonnaise.

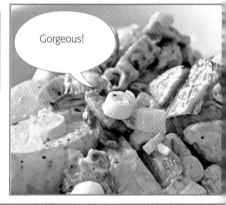

Gorgeous!

Optional Extras: Little pieces of cooked chicken would be lovely thrown in at the end. Chopped cilantro really adds to the flavors and I would recommend using a little if you wish. A lovely alternative to mayonnaise would be sour cream or crème fraîche.

Serving Suggestions: This works well with cold roast chicken, too (see pages 110–11). If you fancy a warm version, put the cooked potatoes in the same pan as the cooked bacon over low heat, add the scallions and replace the mayo with crème fraîche or sour cream. Add some chopped cilantro and serve.

Leftovers: The cooked potatoes will keep on their own in the refrigerator for up to 4 days. Throw them into some simmering water for a couple of minutes just to take the chill out of them. The whole salad will go fairly soggy if kept for long in the refrigerator with the mayonnaise in it, so store the mayonnaise separately if you feel you won't need/eat it all.

CHICKPEA AND RED ONION SALAD SERVES 1

YOU WILL NEED:
- 7 oz (200 g) canned chickpeas
- ½ red onion, chopped finely
- ½ long cucumber, cubed
- 1 garlic clove, peeled and chopped finely
- juice of 1 lemon
- 1 tbsp (15 ml) olive oil

Chickpeas are pale and shaped like hazelnuts. They are the staple ingredient in the delicious hummus dip, and chickpeas with lemon and olive oil are a great marriage. I always buy the ones canned in salted water, they are precooked and don't involve any soaking or general messing around. They are abundantly available. This is a great on-the-go salad to take in for lunch and is very nutritious.

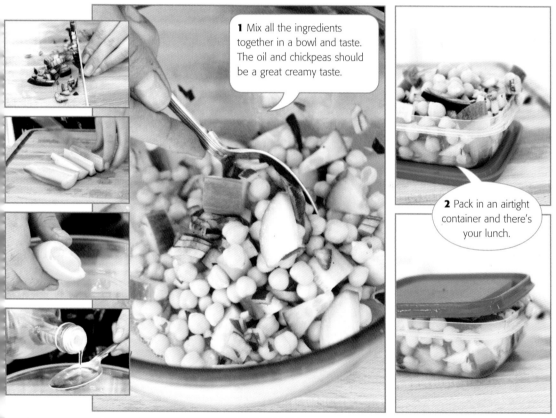

1 Mix all the ingredients together in a bowl and taste. The oil and chickpeas should be a great creamy taste.

2 Pack in an airtight container and there's your lunch.

Optional Extras: Try adding ¼ tsp (1 ml) ground cumin for a totally delicious variation, and scatter in some cold roast chicken (see pages 110–11). Chopped parsley would add a splash of color, while crumbled feta would add an extra twist.
Serving Suggestions: Pack this with some pita bread and it's a very filling lunch. This would be brilliant to serve in a big bowl for a house party, maybe with with some barbecue bits like the honey and mustard chicken (see page 137) or delicious juicy sausages (see page 136). Great with tzatziki as well (see page 61).
Leftovers: This salad will keep in an airtight container in the refrigerator for up to 2 days.

CHICKEN AND TOMATO SALSA WRAP
MAKES 2 WRAPS

In Newcastle, UK, there is a great deli, "Dene's Deli," where a lot of the students go if they cannot be bothered to make lunch, and I have had the same wrap ever since I have been there. It's a whopper wrap with chicken, bacon, avocado, mozzarella, lettuce, mayonnaise and pesto. This wrap recipe, however, is a little simpler and inspired by a true student classic—the fajita!

1 Heat the oil in a skillet, then add the chicken and garlic and lower the heat to medium.

2 Fry the chicken for 2 minutes, then add the bell peppers.

3 Cook for another 3 minutes and check that your chicken is cooked by cutting it open with a knife to make sure there are no traces of pink flesh.

4 Mix the chopped tomato, olive oil and sugar together in a bowl.

5 Take a wrap and spoon the tomato salsa down the center. Repeat with the other wrap.

6 Then add the chicken and red pepper mix.

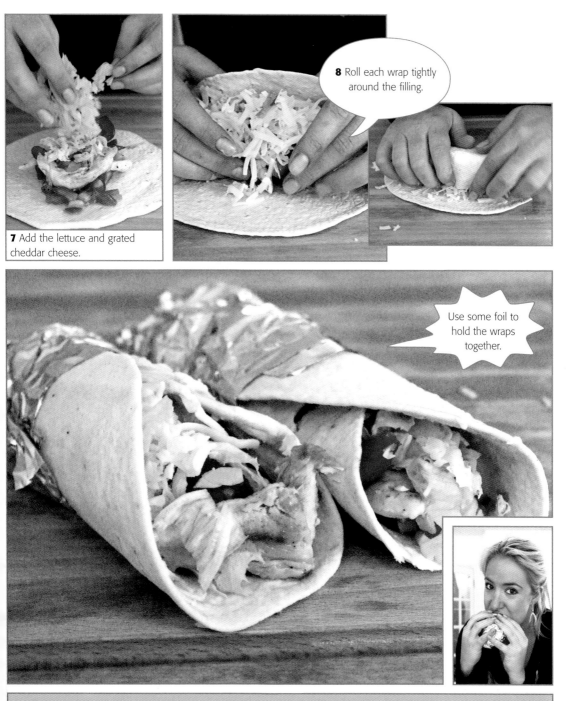

8 Roll each wrap tightly around the filling.

7 Add the lettuce and grated cheddar cheese.

Use some foil to hold the wraps together.

Optional Extras: Grated cheese, lettuce, sour cream, chilies.
Serving Suggestions: Wrap this in foil and take it to university for lunch. Perfect. For more fajita ideas, see page 81.
Leftovers: Keep the cooked chicken mix covered in the refrigerator for up to 2 days. To reheat it, place it in the oven set to 225°F (110°C) for 15 minutes. The tomato salsa will keep in an airtight container in the refrigerator for 2 days.

HOW TO MAKE COUSCOUS SERVES 1

YOU WILL NEED:
¼ cup (50 g) couscous
¼ cup (60 ml) boiling water

Couscous is used extensively in Morocco and the Middle East and is often served with a meat or vegetable stew. It's great eaten on its own, or as an accompaniment. Couscous is amazing with anything from chicken to roasted vegetables. It's perfect for lunch.

1 Put the couscous in a bowl.

2 Pour over the boiling water.

3 Stir well and leave for 5 minutes.

The couscous will now have doubled in weight and more than doubled in size. It can be eaten hot or cold.

4 Mix around with a fork, fluffing it up so all the grains are loose and soft.

Optional Extras: Instead of using boiling water, add some flavor and replace the water with chicken or vegetable stock. You could add 1 tsp (5 ml) of olive oil or butter as well, to add a little flavor if you wish.

Serving Suggestions: Couscous is great with meat such as casseroles and also if you have some spices lying around such as cumin or cardamom. It's good mixed into a salad, too.

Leftovers: Cooked couscous can be kept in a sealed container in your refrigerator for up to 3 days. To reheat it, put it in an ovenproof dish, sprinkle it with a little water and heat it slowly in an oven set to 225°F (110°C). However, it is perfectly good eaten cold.

COUSCOUS WITH RED ROASTED VEGETABLES SERVES 1

Absolutely delicious and nutritious as a salad, great if you're a vegetarian and perfect as a packed lunch. The sweetness of the tomatoes and red bell peppers makes this a true sensation.

YOU WILL NEED:

1 red bell pepper, seeded and sliced
2 tomatoes, halved and quartered
½ red chili, seeded and chopped finely
2 garlic cloves, peeled and crushed
2 tsp (10 ml) olive oil
½ tsp (2 ml) sugar
¼ cup (50 g) couscous
¼ cup (60 ml) boiling water

Preheat the oven to 400°F (200°C).

1 Place the red bell pepper, tomatoes, chili and garlic in a roasting tray, drizzle with the olive oil and sprinkle with the sugar. This really enhances the sweetness in the tomatoes and peppers.

2 Roast for 15 to 20 minutes until the tomatoes and peppers are bursting with juices.

3 Meanwhile, cook the couscous by pouring over the boiling water, leaving it for 5 minutes and then fluffing it up (see opposite).

4 Add the juicy roasted veg to the couscous and either serve now or tip into a packed lunch box for later.

Optional Extras: There is so much you can do with this, and is one of my all-time favorite dishes. You could add all sorts of vegetables to the dish and roast them; red onions would work especially well quartered and roasted with the tomatoes and bell pepper. You could also crumble over some feta cheese, or mozzarella slices, although they can be slightly pricey. You could whip up some pesto, if you have some parsley or basil lying around (see page 65).

Serving Suggestions: A drizzle of balsamic vinegar works wonders with the flavors in this dish. Then tip it all into an airtight container for a perfectly portable packed lunch.

Leftovers: If you have leftovers and want to keep them for another day, I'd recommend storing both items in separate airtight containers in the refrigerator. If they are together the couscous will become really soggy and turn into a big mush. To reheat the veggies, place them in an ovenproof dish and pop into the oven at 225°F (110°C) for 10 minutes.

MOROCCAN COUSCOUS SALAD SERVES 1

Often sold ready-made in supermarkets, this is much more economical and tasty when you make it yourself. I love the combination of the couscous with raisins, cucumber, red onion and yogurt. It makes the thriftiest and tastiest of lunches.

YOU WILL NEED:
1 chicken or vegetable stock cube
¼ cup (60 ml) boiling water
¼ cup (50 g) couscous
½ cucumber, diced
½ red onion, chopped finely
2 tbsp (30 ml) mint, chopped
1 tbsp (15 ml) raisins or currants
1 tbsp (15 ml) olive oil
juice of 1 lemon

2 Fluff up the couscous using a fork, then add the cucumber, red onion, mint and raisins or currants. Add the olive oil and lemon juice, mix well and season with some salt and pepper.

1 Mix the stock cube into the boiling water. Stir well until dissolved and then pour onto the couscous and let stand for 5 minutes.

3 Mix well so that all the flavors are combined.

4 Pack your lunch in an airtight container and on your bike you go …

Optional Extras: A spice would be great here, and I would suggest ¼ tsp (1 ml) cumin to mix with the other ingredients. Chopped cilantro or dried apricots would work well with the flavors here too.
Serving Suggestions: Obviously, these are all ideas of what to take for lunch to university. However, don't think that you can't serve these up for dinner. Use some pita bread as an edible scoop/spoon.
Leftovers: You can mix all the ingredients together and leave them tightly covered in the refrigerator for up to 2 days. This enables all the flavors to intensify and will leave you with a true taste of Morocco.

GREEN COUSCOUS SALAD
SERVES 1

I love this as a really fresh and vibrant salad. Don't overcook the veggies, as they're best with a bit of a crunch, and lots of lime juice. This is so tasty and nutritious to gobble up when you get a minute in your hectic day.

YOU WILL NEED:
- ³/₄ cup (75 g) frozen peas
- 2 oz (50 g) sugar snap peas
- 1 chicken or vegetable stock cube
- ¹/₄ cup (60 ml) boiling water
- ¹/₄ cup (50 g) couscous
- 1 tbsp (15 ml) olive oil
- ½ green chili, seeded and chopped finely
- juice of 1 lime
- 2 oz (50 g) feta cheese

1 Bring a medium saucepan of water to a boil, and add the peas and sugar snap peas. Cook uncovered for 3 to 4 minutes.

2 Meanwhile, mix the stock cube into the boiling water and pour over the couscous. Let stand for 5 minutes, then fluff it up with a fork.

3 Drain the peas and sugar snaps, and add them to the couscous.

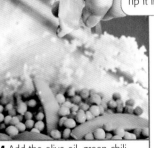

4 Add the olive oil, green chili and lime juice.

5 Mix it all up and have a taste. It should be fresh and vibrant. Tip it into an airtight container.

6 Crumble over the feta and serve.

Optional Extras: Anything green … Try herbs such as cilantro, parsley or basil. Some green bell peppers or a drizzle of pesto would be tasty. What about frozen fava beans or even fresh ones? You could replace the feta with goat cheese.
Serving Suggestions: For lunch I have it just as it is. However, this would be delicious with some roast chicken and is great with a summer barbecue. It tastes best chilled, so put an ice pack in your bag if it's going to be your packed lunch.
Leftovers: If you plan to keep this for longer than a morning, keep the couscous separate from the vegetables. Keep them in airtight containers in the refrigerator for up to 2 days.

4

HEALTHY DAYS FOR THE GIRLS

So, girls, what do we like? For sure the same stuff as the boys now and again, but salads and soups are great for lunch too. I've included some recipes here that are ideal for a girls' night in. A great big stir-fry is always popular. Get everyone to help you with the chopping and throw in some rice or noodles to fill everyone up. Alternatively, you could have a sort of indoor picnic—I love it when my girlfriends come around and sit on the floor tucking into crudités, tzatziki and bruschetta while we gossip. Food like this requires very little cooking and lends the evening a relaxed feel. Easy food for nights when you're all going to sit in front of a movie or just chill with a bottle of wine for a good catch-up chat.

CAESAR SALAD

SERVES 2–4

This is a true tradition in our home. Leftover chicken and bacon seem so lonely and unappealing in the refrigerator, but they're given new life in this salad. If you can, try to make the dressing too—it's a real winner.

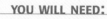

YOU WILL NEED:
1 tbsp (15 ml) olive oil
scant ¼ cup (200 g) diced
    leftover bacon
2 romaine lettuces
2 tbsp (30 ml) Parmesan or
    cheddar cheese

Dressing:
juice of ½ lemon
2 egg yolks
½ tsp (2 ml) mustard
1 tbsp (15 ml) white wine
    vinegar
2 garlic cloves, peeled and
    crushed
1¾ cups (400 ml) olive oil

1 Heat the olive oil in a skillet then add the bacon. Fry for 4 minutes until golden brown. Drain the bacon and set aside.

2 Put the lettuce on a plate and sprinkle over the cheese and bacon.

4 This is the part where you have to be quite careful. DON'T add all the oil at once. Add it bit by bit or it will curdle. Take your time. By the end your dressing should be creamy and smooth.

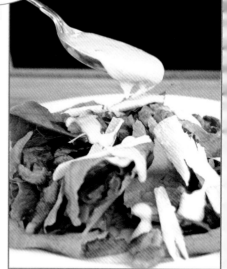

3 To make the dressing, use a whisk or fork to mix the lemon juice, egg yolks and mustard. Slowly add the wine vinegar, mixing well. Then add the garlic.

5 Season with salt and pepper, pour the dressing over the salad and serve.

Optional Extras: Chicken is often used in a Caesar salad, although traditionally it is made without. Don't let this hold you back, however. Feel free to add strips of cooked chicken if you wish. Olives and anchovies would also be delicious.
Serving Suggestions: You could serve this in a big salad bowl and let everyone help themselves.
Leftovers: Keep any bacon or chicken leftovers from anything else for this salad. However, a dressed salad will not keep so if you think your friends won't eat it all, add the dressing to each portion as needed. You could then cover the remaining lettuce leaves, bacon and cheese and keep them in the refrigerator for up to 2 days.

CRUDITÉ SELECTION WITH TZATZIKI **SERVES 2–4**

In French *crudité* means raw. I serve these when I don't feel like cooking and have some friends coming around. It's a Mediterranean feast and always goes down well. A great alternative to potato chips and dip.

YOU WILL NEED:

3 carrots, peeled and cut into sticks

1 cucumber, cut into sticks

10 sugar snap pea pods

10 baby tomatoes

6 pita breads, toasted and sliced

Tzatziki:

6 tbsp (90 ml) plain yogurt

2 tbsp (30 ml) chopped cucumber

2 tsp (10 ml) olive oil

2 tsp (10 ml) lemon juice

1 Chop all the vegetables and toast the pita.

2 Place them on a serving dish.

3 In a small bowl, mix the yogurt, cucumber, olive oil, and lemon juice.

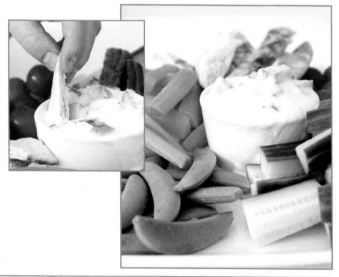

Optional Extras: Radishes are delicious, as are chicory and raw broccoli, which are eaten a lot in France. Adding ½ tsp (2 ml) of ground cumin would be amazing in the tzatziki.

Serving Suggestions: They look so beautiful all on a big serving plate or even in a basket if you have one. You could make more of the tzatziki and put it in a big bowl in the middle so everyone can have a dip.

Leftovers: The raw vegetables will keep for 2 days in the refrigerator, tightly covered, as will the tzatziki.

WARM SALAD NIÇOISE SERVES 2–4

This is a wonderful tasty dish. I love the warmth of the ingredients combined with the crisp crunch of the lettuce leaves. If you are on a bigger budget you might use a tuna steak instead of canned tuna.

YOU WILL NEED:

3 medium eggs

6 baby new potatoes, halved

5 oz (150 g) green beans

4 oz (110 g) lettuce leaves

4 scallions, chopped

18 oz (500 g) canned tuna, drained

2 tbsp (30 ml) olives or anchovies (optional)

Dressing:

6 tbsp (90 ml) olive oil

2 tbsp (30 ml) white wine vinegar

a squeeze of lemon juice

1 Place the eggs in a saucepan of boiling water and cook for 8 minutes.

2 Place the potatoes in a pan of water. Bring to a boil, cook for 5 minutes, then add the beans and cook for another 5 minutes.

4 Drain the potatoes and beans. Scatter the beans over the lettuce.

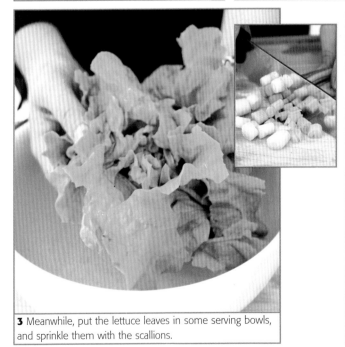

3 Meanwhile, put the lettuce leaves in some serving bowls, and sprinkle them with the scallions.

5 Scatter the tuna onto the salad.

6 Then add the cooked potatoes.

7 Drain the eggs and put them in cold water for 2 minutes to cool. Peel away the shells, then cut the eggs in half and add them to the salad.

8 Carefully arrange the olives or anchovies, if you're using them, over the tuna.

9 Mix the dressing ingredients together and pour over the salad. Add salt and pepper and serve.

Serving Suggestions: Serve with a good hunk of warm bread.

Leftovers: If the salad has been dressed it doesn't keep well at all and wilts very badly. Therefore, if it looks like you will have leftovers, get everyone to add their own dressing and then cover the remaining salad tightly and put it in the refrigerator to eat the next day.

Optional Extras: Olives and anchovies work very well here with the tuna. However, you could add whatever you like, such as tomatoes or cucumber. It's a salad, so just throw in the things you like.

BRUSCHETTA SERVES 2–4

In Italy, bruschetta is also called *fettunata* and this means, "oiled slice." It's absolutely one of my favorite things in the world, and I am such a fan of garlic and all things Italian, so this for me is true heaven, student or not! It's perfect for when you have some friends around and everyone can enjoy it, or you could even have it for a lunch or dinner on your own.

YOU WILL NEED:

4 slices of bread—I use ciabatta
5 garlic cloves, peeled
4 tbsp (60 ml) olive oil
4 tomatoes, halved, seeded
  and flesh chopped
2 tbsp (30 ml) chopped basil

Preheat the broiler.

1 Cut 2 of the garlic cloves in half and rub the cut side of the garlic over the slices of bread. Drizzle with half the olive oil.

2 Place the bread under the broiler to brown for 3 minutes, then turn and continue broiling for another 3 minutes.

3 Meanwhile, finely chop the remaining garlic and mix it with the tomatoes and basil. Pour over the remaining olive oil. Taste and season with salt and pepper, if needed.

4 Remove the bread from the broiler and top with the tomato mixture. Eat immediately.

Optional Extras: Where to start? There is so much you can add to this but it obviously depends on your budget. I love to add avocado slices, mozzarella and a little pesto to it.
Serving Suggestions: It's so delicious as it is, so just enjoy.
Leftovers: The topping will keep on its own, covered and in the refrigerator, for up to 2 days. However, don't leave the actual bruschetta in the refrigerator as the bread will go extremely soggy.

HOMEMADE
PESTO SERVES 4

This is not officially the world's most common student dish; however, at university I am always asked how to make pesto, and I can totally understand why. It's delicious, and a batch will keep in the refrigerator for 4 to 5 days, during which time you can use it on anything from pasta to pizza to bruschetta. It's up to you which herbs to use; I love basil pesto the most, but parsley pesto is very common too.

1 Mix together the parsley, garlic, Parmesan cheese, pine nuts and lemon juice.

3 Taste and season with salt and pepper. If you want it thicker, add some more herbs, or more olive oil if you want it thinner.

2 Then mix in the olive oil.

Optional Extras: This is a list of traditional ingredients for pesto, but if you want to cut costs, leave out the pine nuts.
Serving Suggestions: This is perfect spooned over the top of a bruschetta (see opposite). It's great with pasta as a very easy sauce, and also so delicious with chicken and on pizzas. Try it added to a T Club Sandwich (see page 40).
Leftovers: Keep it tightly covered in the refrigerator for 4 to 5 days. When you use it again make sure you stir it well.

LOW CALORIE VEGETABLE SOUP **SERVES 4**

This is my staple lunch if I am watching my weight. I say this, but it tastes great and would be wrong to put it in the same category as dreadful "diet food." I don't liquidize it, I just put everything into one big pan, and love it über chunky. Perfect as a winter warmer.

YOU WILL NEED:
- 2 vegetable stock cubes
- 4 cups (1 liter) boiling water
- 1 red chili, seeded and chopped roughly
- 2 garlic cloves, peeled and crushed
- 2 carrots, peeled and sliced
- 2 leeks, sliced
- 1 parsnip, peeled and chopped finely
- ½ head of broccoli, cut into florets
- 2 lb (800 g) canned chopped tomatoes
- 1 sprig of rosemary

1 In a pan, stir the stock cubes into the boiling water. Add all the chopped ingredients.

2 Add the tomatoes.

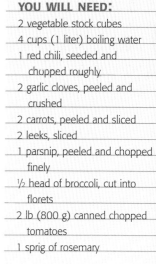

5 You can either liquidize it with a handheld blender or serve it as a really chunky soup with a good hunk of bread.

3 Add the rosemary sprig, hot stock and season with salt and pepper.

4 Put on medium heat and boil for about 30 minutes until all the vegetables are tender.

6 Grind some more pepper over the top and serve.

Optional Extras: Add any vegetables you like; herbs such as basil or parsley are great in this too.
Serving Suggestions: I love this with lots of pepper ground over the top, and that's it.
Leftovers: I find there are leftovers of most soups, but you can keep this in the refrigerator, covered, for up to 3 days. When you want to eat it, bring it briefly to a boil and serve.

TIFF'S HEALTHY MINESTRONE SOUP

SERVES 2–4

I adore minestrone soup, possibly because I'm a fan of chunky soups and this is the king of chunky. The pasta makes it very hearty while the tomatoes add a crucial sweetness. Make a big bowl and let everyone help themselves; for added pleasure, grate some cheese on top.

YOU WILL NEED:

- 2 tbsp (30 ml) olive oil
- scant 1¼ cups diced bacon
- 1 red onion, chopped finely
- 2 garlic cloves, peeled and crushed
- 2 chicken or vegetable stock cubes
- 2 cups (475 ml) boiling water
- 2 carrots, peeled and chopped
- 2 lb (800 g) canned chopped tomatoes
- 7 oz (200 g) dried pasta shells

1 Heat the olive oil in a deep skillet. Fry the bacon, onion and garlic for 4 to 5 minutes until the bacon is starting to brown.

3 Add the carrots, tomatoes and stock to the skillet.

2 Meanwhile, stir the stock cubes into the boiling water.

4 Bring the soup to a boil, then reduce the heat and simmer over medium heat for 15 minutes until all the vegetables are soft. Season with salt and pepper.

5 Add the pasta and cook for another 10 minutes until the pasta is cooked.

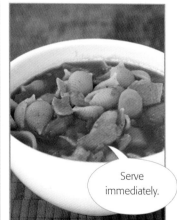

Serve immediately.

Optional Extras: Chopped rosemary would work brilliantly in this, as would a glass of red wine.
Serving Suggestions: Eat with some bread and grate some cheese over the soup.
Leftovers: The soup will keep in the refrigerator for up to 3 days. Before eating it again, bring the soup briefly to a boil and serve piping hot.

HOW TO COOK NOODLES SERVES 2–4

Noodles are absolutely brilliant with all sorts of Asian style meals. It's easy to do a big curry or stir-fry and then have some gorgeous noodles to eat it with. They are great in salads and soups, too. Cooking noodles really depends on which type you choose. Rice noodles are perfect just left in a bowl and covered with boiling water; egg noodles need to be boiled. Hardly rocket science, however.

EGG NOODLES

YOU WILL NEED:

12 oz (350 g) egg noodles

2 Drain and serve, or add to a stir-fry dish (see opposite).

1 Bring a pan of water to a boil, and then add the egg noodles. Cook for 4 minutes.

RICE NOODLES

YOU WILL NEED:

8 oz (225 g) rice noodles

1 Place the noodles in a bowl and cover them with boiling water.

2 Let stand for 5 minutes until soft, then drain and serve, or add to a stir-fry dish (see opposite).

BEEF NOODLE STIR-FRY

SERVES 2–4

If you go to a Chinese restaurant you'll doubtless find a selection of chow mein dishes on the menu. It is the generic term used for a Chinese dish of stir-fried noodles. You could use chicken, vegetables or even small shrimp instead of the beef in this recipe.

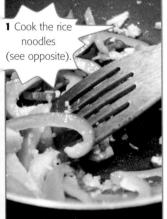

1 Cook the rice noodles (see opposite).

2 Meanwhile, heat the oil in a skillet, then add the chilies, ginger, garlic and green bell pepper. Stir-fry for 4 minutes.

3 Add the beef, lime juice and soy sauce. Fry for a couple of minutes.

4 Add the cooked rice noodles.

5 Mix well and add the honey. Have a taste and add some more soy sauce if you think it needs it.

Optional Extras: Teriyaki sauce instead of the soy sauce is truly delicious and you could use more vegetables if you want.
Serving Suggestions: Serve in a big bowl with a wedge of lime and try eating it with some chopsticks.
Leftovers: This stir-fry will keep in the refrigerator, covered, for up to 2 days. When you want to reheat it, blast it in a wok or skillet until it's piping hot.

SHRIMP AND COCONUT STIR-FRY

SERVES 2–4

I love a good pungent stir-fry—great when you have some friends around. It's easy to find ready-cooked shrimp, so all you have to do is add them at the end. Add a few noodles and you're done.

YOU WILL NEED:
2 tbsp (30 ml) olive oil
½-inch (1 cm) piece of ginger, peeled and chopped finely
3 garlic cloves, peeled and crushed
3 scallions, chopped
1 green chili, chopped
4 tbsp (60 ml) coconut milk
11 oz (285 g) small ready-cooked shrimp
1 tbsp (15 ml) chopped cilantro

1 Heat the oil in a skillet, then add the ginger, garlic, scallions and chili.

2 Fry for 2 minutes, stirring constantly. You should be hit with delicious and fragrant flavors.

4 Right at the end throw in your shrimp.

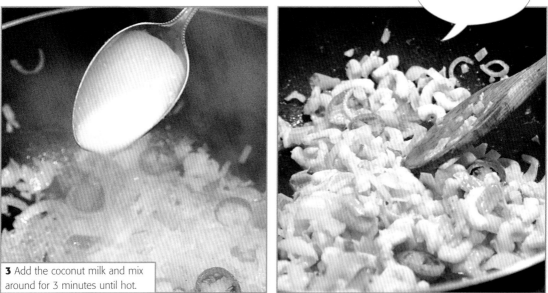

3 Add the coconut milk and mix around for 3 minutes until hot.

Optional Extras: I sometimes like to add some chopped cashews or peanuts to this.
Serving Suggestions: Eat with delicious coconut noodles (see opposite).
Leftovers: Unfortunately this doesn't keep well because of the shrimp. So eat up!

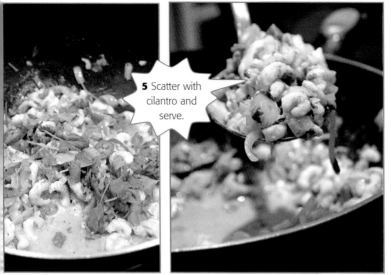

5 Scatter with cilantro and serve.

COCONUT NOODLES

SERVES 2–4

I love this method of cooking noodles. By cooking them in coconut milk, they gain a wonderful fragrant taste.

YOU WILL NEED:

3½ cups (825 ml) coconut milk
12 oz (350 g) egg noodles

1 Pour the coconut milk into a saucepan and bring to a boil.

2 Add the noodles and cook for 4 minutes. Turn the heat off and leave them in the pan to infuse for 5 minutes.

Optional Extras: You could add some sliced ginger to make the flavor stronger and more intense.
Serving Suggestions: I would serve the coconut noodles with a shrimp and coconut stir-fry (see opposite).
Leftovers: You could keep the coconut milk used for boiling the noodles for when you make a curry or stir-fry.
It will keep, covered, in the refrigerator for 2 days.

5

BOYS ARE BACK IN TOWN

This might just be my favorite chapter. I love the student classic: a Mexican feast with tacos and fajitas. It's fun and perfect for a Friday night and it goes without saying that it's definitely not exclusively for boys. Get some tequila shots in and your Friday night will be better than ever. Then for the hangover the next day, there are delicious homemade burgers that you can pile high with cheese and salad. The minute steak sandwich is a favorite for the guys while watching sports, while the hot, hot curry will test you all to see how much spice you can handle. Last but not least you'll find classics like good old sausage and mashed potatoes, and wonderful ways to cook and serve comforting baked potatoes. Enjoy!

HOW TO COOK A BAKED POTATO

SERVES 2

YOU WILL NEED:

2 large white potatoes; ideally use Russet, such as Russet Burbank, or Long White varieties

1 tbsp (15 ml) vegetable oil

A baked potato is a wonderful supper and you can be as adventurous as you like with your filling. Personally, I love ham and cheese—you spoon out the inside, mix it with the cheese and ham, spoon it all back in and stick it under the broiler to brown. It's comfort food at its best. A baked potato might seem very basic; however, when we first moved into our house I was asked by a roommate—no names mentioned—how to cook one, so here's how!

2 Rub the oil over both potatoes and rub in some salt.

1 Preheat the oven to 400°F (200°C). Prick the skin of the potato 3 to 4 times.

3 Bake in the oven for an hour, until crispy. To test if the potatoes are cooked, run a skewer or fork into a potato—it should be lovely and soft.

Optional Extras: If you prefer a less crispy skin, wrap the potatoes in foil. That way they will have a very soft inside and not such a crispy outside. I, however, am a massive fan of the crispy skin.

Leftovers: Cooked baked potatoes can be kept in the refrigerator for 3 days. To reheat, simply heat the oven to 300°F (150°C) and warm them through for 15 minutes.

HAM AND CHEESE BAKED POTATOES

SERVES 4

YOU WILL NEED:

4 large white potatoes

2 tbsp (30 ml) olive oil

scant ½ cup (100 g) butter

7 oz (200 g) ham, chopped

9 oz (250 g) cheddar cheese,
grated, plus extra to top

I love this and I find it such a great way of using up leftover ham and cheese. You create a really delicious filling by spooning out the insides, mixing it with all sorts of ingredients then spooning it all back in. When your work is getting you down, make yourself a baked potato and I am sure all will seem much better.

1 Preheat the oven to 400°F (200°C). Bake the potatoes as described opposite. Set aside for 5 minutes to cool.

2 Cut the potatoes in half and gently scoop out the hot potato inside, leaving the skins intact. Put the insides in a large mixing bowl.

3 Mix the butter, ham and cheese with the potato, and season with salt and pepper. It should be quite creamy and very delicious.

If you don't have a broiler, preheat the oven to 300°F (150°C) and brown the tops.

4 Spoon the filling back into the potato skins and top with more cheese.

5 Place under a hot broiler for 3 to 4 minutes until the cheese is golden.

Optional Extras: A couple of crushed garlic cloves would be delicious added to the ham and cheese, as would some chopped herbs—I would suggest 2 tbsp (30 ml) of chopped rosemary.

Serving Suggestions: Eat with a crisp green salad on the side.

Leftovers: Any leftovers will keep in the refrigerator for 3 days. To reheat, place in the oven at 300°F (150°C) for 15 minutes until hot.

THE CLASSIC— BAKED POTATO WITH BEANS AND CHEESE SERVES 4

YOU WILL NEED:
4 large white potatoes
2 tbsp (30 ml) vegetable oil
2 lb (900 g) baked beans (2 cans)
scant ½ cup (110 g) butter
7 oz (200 g) cheddar cheese, grated

This is such a delicious way to gobble up a baked potato. Warm beans and gorgeously gloopy melting cheese—for me it's food heaven!

1 Preheat the oven to 400°F (200°C). Bake the potatoes (see page 74).

2 Meanwhile, empty the beans into a saucepan and heat on high, stirring all the time until hot. This should take about 5 minutes.

3 Cut the potatoes in half and add the butter.

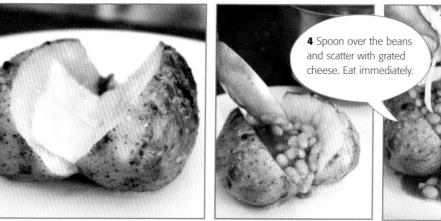

4 Spoon over the beans and scatter with grated cheese. Eat immediately.

Optional Extras: I don't think that this delicious meal needs anything else. However, my friend Bex recommends cottage cheese as a healthy alternative to cheddar. Use 1–2 tbsp (15–30 ml) of cottage cheese per baked potato.
Serving Suggestions: Gobble up on a plate with a good beer.
Leftovers: Beans can be kept in the refrigerator, covered with plastic wrap, for 3 to 4 days. To reheat cook on medium-high, stirring, for 5 minutes till hot. NEVER leave cans open in the refrigerator; tip the contents into a bowl and cover.

SATURDAY MINUTE STEAK SANDWICH

SERVES 2–4

The game is on, boys, and the beers are flowing. So what do you need now? A steak sandwich oozing with mustard and ketchup. Toss a coin to see which one of you will have to make the sandwiches, or, even better, all get involved and try and get it done before kickoff.

YOU WILL NEED:

4 ciabatta rolls

2 tbsp (30 ml) olive oil

2 garlic cloves, halved

1 tbsp (15 ml) vegetable oil

4 minute steaks

4 tsp (20 ml) mustard

4 tomatoes, sliced

3½ oz (100 g) lettuce leaves; arugula leaves work wonders here

Turn on the broiler to high; if you don't have one set the oven to 300°F (150°C).

1 Slice open the rolls, drizzle them with olive oil and rub with the cut side of the garlic cloves.

2 Set under the broiler to crisp up for 5 to 6 minutes, turning halfway through. Set aside.

3 Heat the vegetable oil in a skillet, add the steaks and cook on high heat for 1 to 2 minutes on each side. Remove from the skillet and let rest. They should still be pink in the middle.

5 Add the lettuce leaves, close up the rolls and eat immediately.

4 Spoon 1 tsp (5 ml) of mustard over each roll. Add the tomato slices and then the cooked steaks. Slice the steaks if you wish.

Optional Extras: It's your sandwich so feel free to add ketchup, or to take out the mustard. This is just my take on a steak sandwich but I am very aware that it's a personal thing.

Serving Suggestions: Devour with some chips and a beer.

Leftovers: I don't advise any leftover suggestions as you will have to eat it all—especially if you're boys. Eat up!

MEXICAN FEAST SERVES 2–4

This is the best, most brilliantly fun meal to whip up and eat on a Friday night with some friends before you go out. Delicious fajitas, guacamole, and tacos and maybe a few Mexican drinking games. Watch out, because as soon as your sombreros are on, someone will whip out the tequila and then you've had it. You might not make it to the bar or club. Mexican food consists of fajitas, nachos, quesadillas, guacamole and lots more. You can buy prepared kits in supermarkets now that are very reasonable, but if you make your own you'll probably get more for less money, and of course it'll taste better too.

GUACAMOLE

1 Mix all the ingredients together in a bowl.

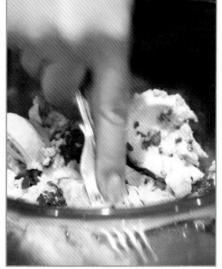

2 Mash the avocados using a fork or masher. Season very well with salt and pepper.

YOU WILL NEED:

2 ripe avocados, peeled, pits removed and sliced
1 red chili, seeded and chopped finely
3 garlic cloves, peeled and crushed
juice of 1 lime
5 tbsp (75 ml) olive oil

Serving Suggestions: This is great with a Mexican feast to accompany fajitas and nachos. However, it's also amazing on a burger (see pages 84–85), or with crudités (see page 61) and potato chips. It's very versatile.
Leftovers: Avocados react with oxygen in the air and go brown very quickly, so if you make this try and use it very quickly or press plastic wrap right onto the surface of the guacamole so there are no air bubbles. You can keep it in the refrigerator but it will go brown quickly.

MEXICAN SPICY TOMATO SALSA

1 Place all the ingredients in a bowl and mix together well. Taste, and season with salt and pepper.

HOT TACOS SERVES 2–4

Amazing, and a real must whenever you're going all Mexican. Taco shells or tortilla chips are so easy to buy. Just add some toppings and away you go.

Preheat the oven to 350°F (180°C).

1 Put the taco shells on a baking sheet. Spoon in the salsa, sour cream and guacamole. Sprinkle with the cheese.

2 Place in the hot oven for 5 to 10 minutes, until the cheese melts. Alternatively, broil them for 5 minutes.

QUESADILLAS
SERVES 2–4

These are what the Mexicans eat as a sandwich, and I'm a mega fan. In Spanish the word translates exactly as "little cheese thing," and the cheese is what makes it so good. You use the same tortillas as you would use for a fajita, so keep some aside if you're making these too. You can cut quesadillas into cute bite-size triangles for party snacks, too.

YOU WILL NEED:
- 4 flour tortillas
- 4 tbsp (60 ml) Guacamole (see page 78)
- 4 tbsp (60 ml) sour cream
- 4 tbsp (60 ml) Mexican Spicy Tomato Salsa (see page 79)
- 9 oz (250 g) cheddar cheese, grated

1 Take 1 tortilla and spread it with half the guacamole, sour cream and salsa, then sprinkle with half the cheese.

Repeat with the second quesadilla.

2 Take another tortilla and sandwich it on top of the one with all the filling. Repeat this with the remaining two tortillas. You will now have two crêpe sandwiches or quesadillas.

3 Heat a skillet over low heat. Warm one quesadilla in the pan for 3 to 4 minutes until brown on one side. Turn it over to brown the other side.

4 Cut each quesadilla into triangles and serve hot.

Incredible.

Optional Extras: You could spice it up by adding some chilies or jalapeños. You could also add some cooked chicken or beef pieces, although I prefer to save the meat for Fajitas (see opposite).

Serving Suggestions: Eat as part of a Mexican meal with tacos and fajitas. If you just want a few light bites then these are great with drinks before you go out, or when you have some friends around and don't want to cook a big meal.

Leftovers: Quesadillas will go soggy in the refrigerator, so try to eat them all up.

FAJITAS SERVES 2–4

This is basically a Mexican wrap made with beef, lots of sauces and some cheese. Serve them hot with some delicious Mexican beer and your evening will be made!

YOU WILL NEED:

1 tbsp (15 ml) vegetable oil
2 garlic cloves, peeled and crushed
4 thin tenderloin steaks, sliced
4 flour tortillas
4 tbsp (60 ml) Mexican Spicy Tomato Salsa (see page 79)
4 tbsp (60 ml) sour cream
4 tbsp (60 ml) Guacamole (see page 78)
4 handfuls shredded iceberg lettuce
9 oz (250 g) cheddar cheese, grated

1 Heat the oil in a skillet, then add the garlic and the steak. Cook over high heat for 3 to 4 minutes. When ready it should still be slightly pink in the middle.

2 Remove from the heat and set aside to rest. Meanwhile, assemble your fajitas.

4 Roll up the wrap, and repeat to make three more fajitas. Delicious.

3 Take one tortilla and spoon over 1 tbsp (15 ml) salsa, followed by the same amount of sour cream and guacamole. Add a few steak slices, then sprinkle with a handful of lettuce and some grated cheese.

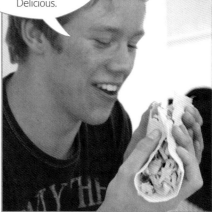

Optional Extras: Try this with fried chicken instead of steak. You could add some sliced, seeded chilies to it too, for a hotter version.

Serving Suggestions: Serve this with a selection of other Mexican dishes, such as Hot Tacos (see page 79) and Quesadillas (see opposite). Wash it down with some Mexican beer, sombreros on your heads and maybe even some Tequila shots to finish.

Leftovers: Not great, so just get eating.

SAUSAGE AND MASH UP

SERVES 2–4

YOU WILL NEED:
10 large white potatoes, such as Russet, chopped roughly
1 tbsp (15 ml) vegetable oil
8 sausages
scant ½ cup (100 g) butter
⅔ cup (150 ml) heavy cream
⅔ cup (150 ml) milk

When I first began university, "mash up" was the term used to describe partying and mashed potato. A weird combination; however, mash was very often consumed on a Friday night before going out partying and eaten with lots of friends, beer and wine. You can add just milk, cream and seasoning to it, but you could also add mustard, pesto, garlic, peas, apricots or cheese. It's so versatile—just remember to season well.

1 Put the potatoes in a large saucepan of water and bring to a boil for about 15 minutes.

2 Meanwhile, heat the oil in a skillet and add the sausages. Cook on medium heat for 10 to 15 minutes until golden brown.

3 Drain the potatoes then put them back in the pan. Mash them until there are no lumps and then add the butter. Mix well and mash in the cream and milk.

4 Taste, and season very well with salt and pepper. Serve with the cooked sausages.

Serving Suggestions: A plate piled high with mash, sausages and a good squeeze of ketchup and mustard.
Leftovers: Cold cooked sausages will keep in the refrigerator for 3 days and are great eaten cold. To reheat them, place them in a skillet over medium heat for 5 minutes.

MASHED POTATO VARIATIONS SERVES 2–4

As I mention above, the additions to mashed potato are endless. Here are a few of my favorites.

Mustard Mash
Using the recipe opposite, add 3 tbsp (45 ml) dijon mustard with the milk and cream.

Pea Mash
This is an Irish recipe and is wonderful as an accompaniment or just eaten on its own.

Pesto Mash
Add 3 tbsp (45 ml) pesto (see page 65) with the butter and do not add the cream or milk.

Cheesy Mash
Add generous 1 cup (110 g) grated cheese with the milk and cream.

Garlic Mash
Add 3 crushed garlic cloves to the mash along with the milk and cream.

1 Bring a pan of water to a boil and add 2²/₃ cups (300 g) frozen peas. Cook for 5 minutes. Drain and add the peas to the mash along with the cream and milk.

Optional Extras: Add 2 tbsp (30 ml) of finely chopped rosemary and/or 2 peeled, crushed garlic cloves to the plain mash along with the milk and cream.

HOMEMADE BEEF BURGERS WITH RUSTIC FRIES

MAKES 4 BURGERS

Preheat the oven to 400°F (200°C).

1 Cut the potatoes into wedges; you should get 4–6 wedges from each potato. Place them on a baking sheet, drizzle with half the olive oil and season with salt.

2 Cook in the oven for 20 to 30 minutes until golden brown and soft.

3 Meanwhile, mix the beef with the onion, garlic, chili, parsley and 1 tbsp (15 ml) olive oil. Use your hands to divide the mixture into 4, then shape into burgers about 1 inch (2.5 cm) thick.

4 Heat the remaining oil in a skillet and add the burgers. Cook on medium heat for 5 minutes. Turn and cook for another 5 minutes. The burgers should be brown on the outside and cooked through, with hardly any trace of pink inside. After 10 to 12 minutes they should be ready.

5 Add 2 slices of cheese to the top of each burger, just before they're ready.

6 Assemble the burgers by sandwiching a few lettuce leaves, a burger, a tomato slice and a squirt of ketchup and mayonnaise in each bun.

Serve with the hot fries—yum!

Optional Extras: Place a cube of cheese—I like cheddar, or even blue cheese—inside the beef mixture. Do this once you have shaped them into burgers and before you cook them. Then when you take a bite you'll get melted cheese inside your cooked burger—amazing. Or place a slice of cheese on each burger 2 minutes before they are ready and watch it melt over your delicious burgers. In the summer, sundried tomatoes are delicious added to the mixture.

Serving Suggestions: I love to have my burger in a bun with ketchup, cheese on top, lettuce, tomato and a spot of mayo. Guacamole (see page 78) is also gorgeous, as are fried bacon and some fried onions. Up to you entirely.

Leftovers: Leave the raw mixture in the refrigerator for up to a day and then shape and cook. If you have some leftover raw mixture and you don't want to make another burger, form it into little balls to make your own meatballs. Cook in a pan and serve with spaghetti and tomato and garlic sauce (see page 27).

HOT, HOT LAMB CURRY SERVES 4

How brave are you? This curry is punchy and spicy, perfect for a lads' night in with a few beers. It is very spicy, so if you want to tone it down leave out the pepper flakes and use a couple of green chilies instead.

1 Mix the lamb, yogurt, turmeric and cumin together in a bowl. Put in the refrigerator for an hour to marinate.

2 Heat the oil in a large pan and fry the onion, garlic and ginger.

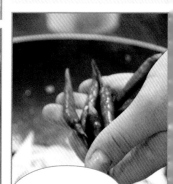

3 Add the chilies and red pepper flakes and mix around.

5 Mix up the boiling water and stock cubes, then pour over the lamb. Cook over low heat for 35 minutes until the lamb is tender.

4 Add the yogurt-marinated lamb, stir well and season with salt and pepper.

6 Add the spinach and cook for another 5 minutes.

7 Serve hot, hot, hot with a dollop of yogurt to cool the flames!

Optional Extras: Feel free to use coconut milk instead of stock here. Red chilies would also be great and give the dish some extra color.

Serving Suggestions: Serve with some buttered basmati rice with cilantro (see page 125), some naan bread and a good mango chutney.

Leftovers: You can reheat the curry the following day by slowly bringing it to a boil in a pan set over low heat. Alternatively, it can be frozen for up to 2 months.

6

TIFF'S TUESDAYS

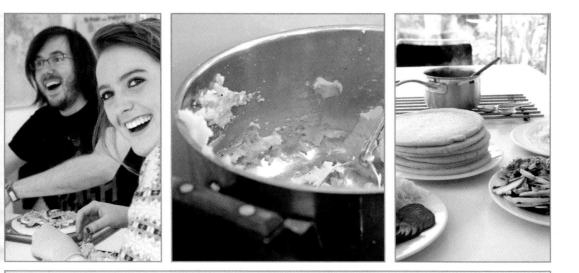

What are Tiff's Tuesdays? They began in my second year at university after I had a few people around for supper one Tuesday. My friends asked if this could happen weekly. I was delighted; however, like all students with an eye on my bank balance, I suggested that they each contribute a few dollars for the meal. They all agreed and it was a done deal—Tiff's Tuesdays were born.

This chapter has some recipes to help you prepare your own thrifty midweek feast. Don't feel rude asking people to contribute—it's all part of it. It's good food that will make your Tuesdays seem better than they have ever been.

HOW TO COOK PIZZA

One Tuesday at university my friends all called me up and said they were broke due to it being end of term. I quietly checked my cupboards and explored what I had after a term of buying all sorts of bits. I found a can of tomatoes, an onion and some cheese in the refrigerator. Pizza was screaming out at me. The secret here is a hot, hot oven so your pizza gets a wonderful crisp crust. You can buy pizza bases very easily. You can create your own toppings and of course make your own delicious tomato sauce too.

BASIC TOMATO SAUCE FOR PIZZA

MAKES ENOUGH FOR 4 PIZZAS

YOU WILL NEED:
- 4 tbsp (60 ml) butter
- 2 garlic cloves, peeled, chopped and crushed
- ½ onion, chopped finely
- 1¼ lb (600 g) canned chopped tomatoes
- 1 tsp (5 ml) sugar
- 1 tsp (5 ml) dried oregano

1 Melt the butter in a pan.

2 Add the garlic and onions. Cook on medium heat for 3 to 4 minutes until soft.

4 On medium-low heat, cook for up to half an hour to get all the delicious, intense flavors. Set aside until you're ready to assemble your pizza.

3 Add the tomatoes and the sugar. Season with salt and pepper and add the oregano.

Optional Extras: I often use a red onion instead of a white one as it's just a bit different. You could also add 1 tsp (5 ml) tomato paste, which has a much more concentrated tomato flavor. Also feel free to throw in some fresh tomatoes. I would suggest using 4–6 halved small tomatoes.

Serving Suggestions: Delicious as your base for pizza. Just add a little bit of sliced mozzarella and basil and you have the perfect Italian pizza.

Leftovers: This will keep in an airtight container in the refrigerator for 3 days. To reheat it, slowly bring it to a boil in a pan.

PIZZA MARGHERITA MAKES 4

This is very simple and made with just tomato and cheese. The secret is to use a lot of cheese so that when you take a bite, you end up with cheese strings everywhere. If you don't have four baking sheets, you can always flip over some roasting trays and use them instead (see step 2).

YOU WILL NEED:
4 pizza bases
8 tbsp (120 ml) Basic Tomato Sauce for Pizza (see opposite)
12 oz (350 g) mozzarella, sliced thinly
18 oz (500 g) cheddar cheese, grated
4 tsp (20 ml) dried oregano (optional)

Preheat the oven to 400°F (200°C).

2 Place 3–4 slices of mozzarella on each pizza.

3 Then scatter with grated cheese. Season well and if you have it, sprinkle 1 tsp (5 ml) of dried oregano over each pizza.

1 Put the pizza bases on baking sheets and spread each one with 2 tbsp (30 ml) of the tomato sauce.

4 Put the pizzas in the hot oven for 15 to 20 minutes.

You want the pizza base to be golden and crispy, and the cheese should be a little crispy too.

Optional Extras: The list is endless! You could add some ham to the pizza topping, or some pepperoni, mushrooms, black olives, bell peppers, anchovies …

Serving Suggestions: Having taken it out of the oven, I would serve this with a drizzle of olive oil and maybe a few torn up basil leaves for extra color and flavor.

Leftovers: I hate reheated pizza as it goes all soggy; however, it's a great snack eaten cold, so leave it in the refrigerator and eat it for lunch the next day.

MY PERFECT PIZZA MAKES 4

This is my favorite pizza topping. I adore anchovies but I know that a lot of my friends find that weird, so I have left them out, but if you are like me and love them, add 2–3 anchovy fillets to the topping.

YOU WILL NEED:
- 4 pizza bases
- 8 tbsp (120 ml) Basic Tomato Sauce for Pizza (see page 90)
- 9 oz (250 g) mushrooms, sliced
- 9 oz (250 g) ham, sliced
- 12 oz (350 g) mozzarella, sliced thinly
- 18 oz (500 g) cheddar cheese, grated
- 4 tsp (20 ml) dried oregano (optional)

> Preheat the oven to 400°F (200°C).

1 Put the pizza bases on baking sheets and spread each one with 2 tbsp (30 ml) of the sauce.

2 Arrange the mushrooms, ham, mozzarella and cheddar. Scatter with dried oregano, if you're using it.

3 Put them in the hot oven for 15 to 20 minutes until golden brown and bubbling.

Optional Extras: Anchovies are perfect with this, as are black olives. You could use prosciutto or Serrano ham instead of the ordinary ham; however, they will be more expensive.
Serving Suggestions: Delicious with a drizzle of chili oil over the top. Make your own by pouring olive oil into a jar with 3–4 sliced red chilies. Leave it for up to a month to mature. Great also with a handful of arugula leaves over the top.

HOT AND SPICY PIZZA SERVES 4

I know that when I have made pizzas for friends in the past they love a good spicy version. Therefore this is brilliant to do, especially if you're making it for boys; you can see how much spice they can take.

YOU WILL NEED:
4 pizza bases
8 tbsp (120 ml) Basic Tomato Sauce for Pizza (see page 90)
9 oz (250 g) hot pepperoni, sliced
12 slices of preserved red or green jalapeños, drained
18 oz (500 g) cheddar cheese, grated
4 tsp (20 ml) chili oil (optional)

Preheat the oven to 400°F (200°C).

2 Scatter a quarter of the pepperoni slices and the jalapeños over each pizza. Finish off with the cheese and chili oil, if you're using it.

1 Put the pizza bases on baking sheets and spread each one with 2 tbsp (30 ml) of the sauce.

3 Cook in the oven for 15 to 20 minutes until golden brown.

Optional Extras: Depends how far you want to go. Feel free to throw on some more jalapeños.
Serving Suggestion: When it comes out of the oven drizzle the pizza with some more chili oil.

VEGETARIAN PASTA HEAVEN

SERVES 6

I dedicate this recipe to my friend Greg, who is a devoted vegetarian. When I was much younger he used to come for dinner and I started experimenting with vegetarian recipes. Whether you're veggie or not, I thoroughly recommend this dish. I started making it when I was 16 and it's always worked wonderfully.

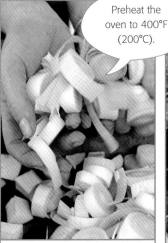

Preheat the oven to 400°F (200°C).

1 Put the eggplant, leeks and red onions in a large roasting tray.

2 Drizzle with 2 tbsp (30 ml) of the olive oil. Mix well and roast in the oven for 15 minutes.

3 Add the bell peppers, tomatoes and herbs to the part-cooked vegetables.

4 Mix well, season with salt and pepper, and add another tbsp (15 ml) of olive oil if it looks a little dry. Return the roasting tray to the oven for another 15 minutes.

5 Meanwhile, bring a large pan of water to a boil. Add the pasta and simmer for 10 minutes or according to the package directions.

6 Mix together the parsley, 3 tbsp (45 ml) of olive oil and the garlic to make a gorgeous pesto-type sauce.

7 Drain the pasta and return it to the pan. Stir in the butter.

8 Remove the roasted vegetables from the oven and tip them onto the pasta.

10 Season with salt and pepper and stir in the mascarpone. It should taste sensational— creamy, garlicky and yet full of goodness with the roasted vegetables.

9 Stir in the pesto-type sauce and mix well.

Serve immediately.

Optional Extras: If you want to add some meat I'd suggest some cooked chicken strips, or even some chopped bacon.
Serving Suggestions: Delicious with a lovely green salad of lettuce, scallions and avocado.
Leftovers: The roasted vegetables will keep, covered, in the refrigerator for 3 days and can be eaten cold in a salad or even as a topping for a pizza. Reheat in the oven at 300°F (150°C) for 15 minutes. The actual pasta dish will keep in the refrigerator in an airtight container for 3 days. To reheat it, place it in a saucepan over medium heat for 5 to 8 minutes and stir in 1 tsp (5 ml) of olive oil.

LASAGNA SERVES 6

This is a genuine staple and a truly gorgeous dish. There are three stages to it: the meat sauce, the cheese sauce and then assembling it. Oh, and maybe eating it should be the fourth stage!

Preheat the oven to 400°F (200°C).

1 Heat the olive oil in a large pan and cook the garlic, onion and chili over medium heat. Cook for 5 minutes until soft.

2 Add the beef and cook on high heat for 3 to 4 minutes until the beef is brown.

3 Add the ketchup and tomatoes. Season and simmer over low heat for at least an hour.

4 Meanwhile, make the cheese sauce. Put the butter and flour in a pan, and cook on medium heat, stirring, for 1 to 2 minutes.

This is called a roux and will help to thicken the sauce.

5 Gradually whisk in the milk. Any lumps should dissolve as the milk becomes thicker. Stir for 4 to 5 minutes.

6 Taste and season with salt and pepper, then add the cheese. Mix well until the cheese dissolves.

7 Grease a large lasagna dish with butter.

8 Then lay about 4 pasta sheets on the bottom of the dish.

Break a sheet up and use the pieces to fill in the gaps—this applies all the way through.

9 Spread 3 tbsp (45 ml) of meat sauce over the pasta and repeat with the cheese sauce.

10 Assemble your next layer of pasta over the cheese sauce and repeat the process. You should be able to assemble 3–4 layers of pasta, depending on the size of your dish.

11 Sprinkle the top with grated cheese.

12 Cook in the oven for 35 to 45 minutes until golden brown.

Delish!

Optional Extras: You could substitute the meat sauce with roasted vegetables to make a vegetable lasagna. Turn to the recipe for Vegetarian Pasta Heaven (see page 94) for the way to cook them. If you want a bit of extra flavor, add ½ tsp (2 ml) of grated nutmeg to the cheese sauce along with the milk.

Serving Suggestions: Serve with a delicious green salad or some garlic bread (see page 99).

Leftovers: Lasagna will keep uncooked and assembled in the refrigerator for 2 days, so you can make it well in advance. Once cooked, it will keep in the refrigerator for 3 days. To reheat, place in the oven at 300°F (150°C) for 15 minutes, or until piping hot. Use any leftover meat sauce for spaghetti bolognese, or shepherd's pie. Any leftover cheese sauce could be reused in cauliflower cheese (see pages 36–37) or a gooey leek gratin (see page 115).

SPAGHETTI BOLOGNESE
SERVES 6

My dad makes the most sensational Spaghetti Bolognese. The secret is to let it bubble for as long as possible. The Italians cook it for 3 to 4 hours and it's even better reheated the next day. Spaghetti Bolognese is traditionally a student favorite. I absolutely adore it.

YOU WILL NEED:
- 4 tbsp (60 ml) olive oil
- 4 garlic cloves, peeled and crushed
- 1 onion, peeled and chopped
- 1 red chili, seeded and chopped
- 9 oz (250 g) mushrooms, sliced
- 2¼ lb (1 kg) lean ground beef
- 2 glasses of red wine
- 1 tbsp (15 ml) tomato ketchup
- 2 lb (900 g) canned tomatoes
- 2 tbsp (30 ml) dried oregano (optional)
- 18 oz (500 g) dried spaghetti
- handful grated cheddar cheese

1 Heat the olive oil in a large saucepan over medium heat and add the garlic, onion and chili. Cook for 5 minutes until soft.

2 Add the mushrooms and beef. Season with salt and pepper. Cook on high heat, for 3 to 4 minutes until most of the meat is brown but there is still a sign of pink—this will stop it becoming too tough.

3 Add the red wine and ketchup, stirring well, then add the tomatoes and oregano, if you're using it.

4 Let the sauce bubble on low heat for as long as time allows—ideally at least 1½ hours.

5 Bring a large saucepan of water to a boil and drop in the spaghetti, stirring until it is all submerged. Simmer for 10 minutes, or according to the package directions. Drain the pasta then serve it topped with the hot bolognese sauce.

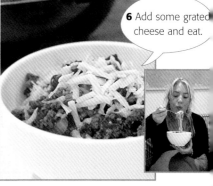

6 Add some grated cheese and eat.

Optional Extras: You could add some bacon for a meatier taste. You could also serve penne pasta with this; mix the cooked penne and bolognese together and place in an ovenproof dish, sprinkled with lots of grated cheese, then place in the oven at 350°F (180°C) for 15 minutes until the cheese is deliciously brown and bubbly.

Serving Suggestions: Serve with some garlic bread (see opposite), a side salad and a glass of red wine.

Leftovers: Bolognese sauce keeps wonderfully well in the refrigerator for 3 days. To reheat, place in a saucepan and slowly bring to a boil. It also freezes very well for up to 3 months. To defrost, leave it in the refrigerator overnight and then heat it in a saucepan until piping hot.

GARLIC BREAD

SERVES 6

Garlic Bread is amazing with lasagna, spaghetti bolognese or shepherd's pie. It's comfort food at its absolute best and definitely worth the effort.

YOU WILL NEED:
- 1³/₄ cups (400 g) soft butter
- 8 garlic cloves, peeled and crushed
- 3 tbsp (45 ml) parsley, chopped
- 2 French baguettes

Preheat the oven to 350°F (180°C).

2 Take the baguettes and slice into them at regular intervals along their length. DON'T cut all the way through, however.

3 Fill each pocket with 1 heaped tsp (5 ml) of garlic butter.

1 Mix the butter, garlic, and parsley together in a bowl. Season with salt and pepper.

If there is any left over, spread it over the top of the baguettes.

4 Wrap each baguette in foil and place in the hot oven for 15 to 20 minutes.

Optional Extras: You could use rosemary or even sage if you want an alternative to parsley.
Serving Suggestions: This is an imperative with spaghetti bolognese or lasagna.
Leftovers: Not great, as it does go quite soggy once cooked.

SHEPHERD'S PIE
SERVES 6

This is so delicious, especially on winter days. You can have it with some delicious peas and a good blob of ketchup. No clues with the name, but Shepherd's Pie is made with lamb and Cottage Pie with beef, so if you prefer beef then just substitute ground beef for the ground lamb.

YOU WILL NEED:

4 tbsp (60 ml) olive oil

4 garlic cloves, peeled and crushed

1 red chili, seeded and chopped finely

1 red onion, peeled and chopped

3 carrots, peeled and chopped

2¼ lb (1 kg) lean ground lamb

3 tbsp (45 ml) Worcestershire sauce

2 glasses of red wine

14 oz (400 g) canned chopped tomatoes

9 oz (250 g) cheddar cheese, grated

Potato Topping:

3½ lb (1.6 kg) potatoes, peeled

½ cup (110 g) butter

¾ cup (175 ml) milk

Preheat the oven to 400°F (200°C).

1 Heat the olive oil in a large saucepan over medium heat and add the garlic, chili, onion and carrots. Cook on medium-low heat for 4 to 5 minutes until soft.

2 Raise the heat and when the vegetables are soft add the lamb.

3 Cook for 4 to 5 minutes

4 Add the Worcestershire sauce, wine, and tomatoes. Season well.

5 Cook for up to 1 hour, longer if you can. It should taste very meaty and delicious.

6 While the meat is bubbling away, bring a large pan of water to a boil and add the potatoes. Cook until soft, around 15 to 20 minutes, depending on their size.

7 Drain and mash well, add the butter and milk and season with salt and pepper.

8 Spoon in the meat sauce into a large ovenproof dish.

It should fill half the dish.

9 Carefully spoon the mashed potato over the top.

10 Season, then sprinkle with grated cheddar cheese.

11 Place on a baking sheet in the oven for 30 to 40 minutes until golden and bubbling.

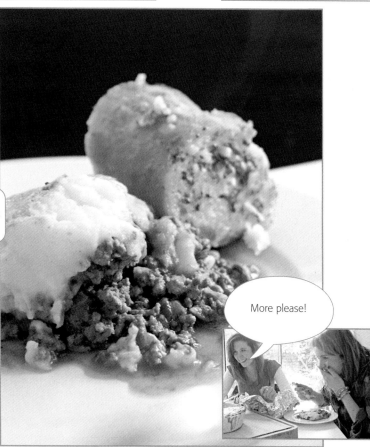

More please!

Optional Extras: You could use Gruyère cheese as a treat for the top, as it's sensational when melted. You could also use celery instead of (or as well as) the carrots.

Serving Suggestions: Amazing with peas, ketchup and a glass of red wine.

FISH PIE SERVES 6

I love, love Fish Pie. It's creamy, rich, utterly good comfort food on a plate. There's nothing better, no matter what the season. We were incredibly lucky at university because we were literally 20 minutes away from the coast and everything from oysters to cod was sold at amazing prices. We also had a brilliant fish supplier. The fish was fresh, fresh, fresh! Try and be thrifty with your money and shop around for the best fish. Use markets and fish suppliers as they have such a wide and fresh range.

> Preheat the oven to 350°F (180°C).

1 Bring a large pan of water to a boil and add the potatoes. Cook for 15 to 20 minutes until soft.

2 Drain and mash, mix in the butter and season well. Set aside.

> Get your fish supplier to skin the fish for you.

> The fish should become opaque and a little flaky.

3 Put the shrimp and fish in a saucepan with the garlic, milk and cream. Cook on medium heat for 5 to 10 minutes until the fish is opaque and cooked through. Taste the sauce and season it with salt and pepper as you like.

4 Use a slotted spoon to remove the fish from the pan and place it in a large ovenproof dish.

5 Slowly bring the milk mixture to a boil. Cook for 3 to 4 minutes, stirring regularly, until it has thickened a little.

6 Scatter the fish with the scallions then pour over the sauce.

If it's looking too dry, then feel free to add a little more cream or milk.

7 Arrange the egg slices over the pie. Sprinkle with parsley and season with salt and pepper.

8 Spoon the mashed potato onto the pie, then sprinkle with cheese.

9 Place on a baking sheet in the oven for 30 to 40 minutes until golden and bubbling.

Optional Extras: Feel free to use the kind of fish you like. Cod is very reasonable, as is haddock—I love the smoky flavor of haddock. Salmon is delicious in this as well.

Serving Suggestions: Perfect with green peas, a bottle of dry white wine and a whole load of friends.

Leftovers: Since this dish includes ready-cooked shrimp in the ingredients, it's not something you should try to keep and then reheat. If you make it without the shrimp, however, you can keep it for up to 2 days.

THAI FISHCAKES

SERVES 6

Not only fresh and fragrant but also an economical choice, Thai fishcakes are so easy to make and they're great to give your friends. Serve them with some sweet chili sauce and a big green salad for a healthy and very simple meal. Make sure everyone brings their own booze and get them to contribute for the shopping so the cook isn't left short-changed.

Chop all the ingredients.

If you have a handheld blender you can use it to combine the ingredients even more. A chunkier version is fine, however.

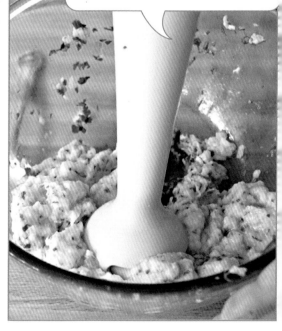

1 Combine the fish, scallions, chilies, garlic, ginger, cilantro, limes and sweet chili sauce.

2 Take 1 tbsp (15 ml) of the mixture and shape it into a fishcake using your hands. If the mixture seems too dry add a little more lime juice, and if it's very wet sprinkle about 1 tbsp (15 ml) of all-purpose flour over your hands to help shape the patties.

You should be able to make about 12 fishcakes from the mixture.

3 Heat the oil in a skillet and add the fishcakes. You may need to cook them in batches if your skillet is small.

4 Fry them over medium heat for 4 to 5 minutes on each side until golden. Serve hot.

Serving Suggestions: Sweet chili sauce is a great dipping sauce, or try soy sauce mixed with a little honey. Great with a big green salad and some boiled potatoes. Perfect for a night in with all your friends.

Leftovers: Cook the fishcakes as soon as you make them or keep them raw in the refrigerator to cook later that day.

TUSCAN BAKED CHICKEN

SERVES 6–8

I did this quite recently for a supper party and it went down wonderfully. I love recipes where you just toss everything in, throw it into the oven and that's that. Ideal as well if you have people coming for supper, and then you can just go and get ready when it's all in the oven.

YOU WILL NEED:

- 4 chicken thighs
- 4 chicken legs
- 6 garlic cloves, peeled and bruised
- 4 lemons, quartered
- 4 tbsp (60 ml) olive oil
- 1 glass of white wine (optional)
- 3 rosemary sprigs, snipped
- 2 red onions, peeled and quartered

Preheat the oven to 350°F (180°C).

1 Put the chicken and garlic in a large ovenproof dish.

2 Squeeze the lemon quarters over the chicken and then tuck the lemon quarters into the dish.

3 Pour over the olive oil. Add the white wine if you're using it.

4 Throw in the rosemary and red onions.

5 Cook in the oven for 20 minutes. Serve hot.

Optional Extras: You could add all sorts of vegetables; tomatoes would be delicious and all sorts of herbs.
Serving Suggestions: To keep with the Italian theme I like to serve this with some pesto (see page 65), gorgeous spaghetti and a salad. It's just so easy.
Leftovers: Keep any leftovers to eat cold in a salad the next day.

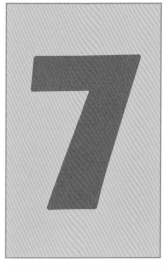

7

WASTED WEEKENDS

At university, weekends are usually a time for a massive chill out. There's always one highlight of the weekend: dinner. When the wind is howling and the rain is pouring there is nothing like huddling around a table for a big dinner with all the trimmings. Weekends give you time to do this and it can be fun preparing all the bits then chilling out with your friends before you all sit down to eat.

Weekends are also a great time to make stews and casseroles—great whether you're eating in front of the TV or have a few people coming around for dinner. Just cook them in the morning and leave them until you're ready to eat that night.

PERFECT ROAST CHICKEN SERVES 4

Sweet, juicy and tender roast chicken stuffed with garlic, lemon and a good bit of butter. It's gorgeous with roasted vegetables, but you could also serve it warm with lots of salads in the summer.

YOU WILL NEED:

4 lb (1.8 kg) whole chicken

scant 1 cup (200 g) butter

1 garlic bulb, cut in half horizontally

1 lemon, halved

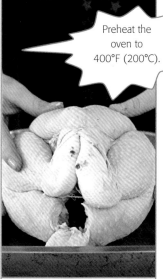

Preheat the oven to 400°F (200°C).

1 Put the raw chicken in a roasting tray.

2 Cut the butter into chunks and rub it over the skin on the top of the chicken. Fit some of the butter in the cavities between the legs and the wings.

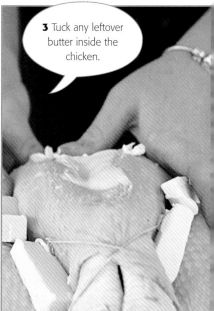

3 Tuck any leftover butter inside the chicken.

4 Tuck half of the garlic inside the chicken.

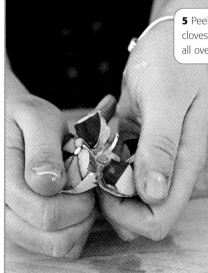

5 Peel and lightly crush the cloves from the other half. Rub all over the chicken skin.

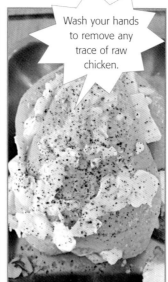

Wash your hands to remove any trace of raw chicken.

6 Tuck a lemon half inside the chicken and squeeze the other half over the outside.

7 Cover the chicken with foil and put it in the oven. It will need 20 minutes for every 18 oz (500 g), plus an additional 20 minutes. So, a 4 lb (1.8 kg) bird will take 1½ hours. Remove the foil after an hour to let the skin brown.

8 Once you have removed the foil, baste the chicken with the cooking juices from time to time. Just spoon them over and quickly return it to the oven.

9 Remove the chicken from the oven and place it on a carving board while you make the gravy (see page 112). Resting it for 10 to 15 minutes will also make it easier to carve.

Optional Extras: Herbs such as sage, rosemary or thyme are delicious chopped and rubbed all over the buttered skin and stuffed inside the chicken. A glass of white wine is delicious poured into the roasting tray before you place it in the oven. It steams the chicken, keeping it moist, and intensifies the flavors.

Serving Suggestions: Serve with delicious crispy roast potatoes (see page 113), gravy (see page 112) and a selection of vegetables, such as Gooey Leek Gratin (see page 115).

Leftovers: There is so much you can do with roast chicken. Keep the meat and use it in a salad, like Caesar salad (see page 60), or toss it into a carbonara pasta sauce for a delicious twist on pasta carbonara (see page 29). Use the leftover meat for a sandwich, or even a stir-fry with some noodles. You can keep it in the refrigerator, covered, for 2 days.

GORGEOUS GRAVY

SERVES 4

A delicious roast chicken requires a really delicious gravy. It only takes a few minutes and can be done while the cooked chicken is resting. I like to add some white wine and use as much of the chicken juices as possible.

YOU WILL NEED:

chicken juices from a roast chicken (see pages 110–111)
2 chicken stock cubes
2 cups (500 ml) boiling water
1 glass of white wine
2 tbsp (30 ml) all-purpose flour
2 tbsp (30 ml) butter

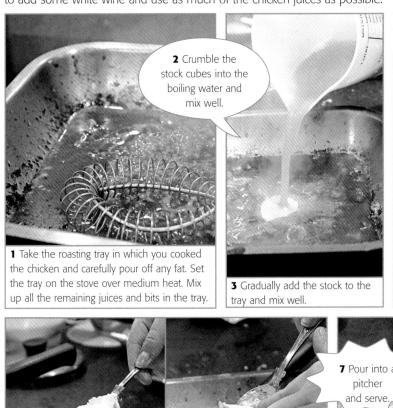

2 Crumble the stock cubes into the boiling water and mix well.

1 Take the roasting tray in which you cooked the chicken and carefully pour off any fat. Set the tray on the stove over medium heat. Mix up all the remaining juices and bits in the tray.

3 Gradually add the stock to the tray and mix well.

4 Add the wine and season with salt and pepper.

7 Pour into a pitcher and serve.

5 The gravy will be quite thin, so add the flour and butter to thicken it slightly. If you want it really thick, double the amount of flour and butter. Stir well and bring it back to a simmering point.

6 Let it bubble for 3 minutes, then taste and season with salt and pepper.

Optional Extras: Add some herbs, such as a couple of rosemary sprigs or thyme, for extra flavor.
Leftovers: I often find myself with some leftover gravy. You can keep it in the refrigerator for 2 days and reheat it in a saucepan for 5 minutes until piping hot.

INGRID'S ROAST POTATOES SERVES 6

Crispy roast potatoes are a staple part of a roast dinner. They are amazing, but there is an art to getting them right. My best friend makes the best crispy, fluffy roasts and this is the way she does it. They take a while to cook, so remember to start them in plenty of time.

YOU WILL NEED:
8 white potatoes, cut into
    2-inch (5 cm) pieces
4 tbsp (60 ml) olive oil
4 tbsp (60 ml) butter
2 tbsp (30 ml) chopped
    rosemary (optional)

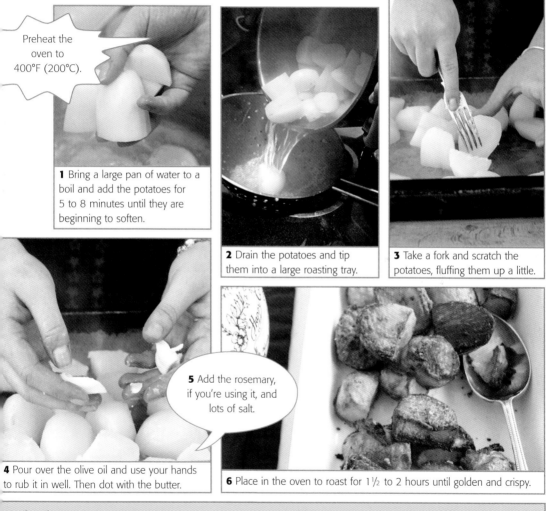

Preheat the oven to 400°F (200°C).

1 Bring a large pan of water to a boil and add the potatoes for 5 to 8 minutes until they are beginning to soften.

2 Drain the potatoes and tip them into a large roasting tray.

3 Take a fork and scratch the potatoes, fluffing them up a little.

5 Add the rosemary, if you're using it, and lots of salt.

4 Pour over the olive oil and use your hands to rub it in well. Then dot with the butter.

6 Place in the oven to roast for 1½ to 2 hours until golden and crispy.

Optional Extras: I love cooking these with goose fat. It's a brilliant way to roast potatoes and gets them so crunchy and gorgeous. Just replace the olive oil with goose fat.
Serving Suggestions: Perfect with roast chicken (see pages 110–111) and all the trimmings.
Leftovers: Keep the cooked potatoes and eat them cold in a tuna or chicken salad. They will keep, covered, in the refrigerator for 2 to 3 days. To reheat, place in the oven at 250°F (130°C) for 15 minutes.

BUTTERED BROCCOLI SERVES 6

When I was taught to cook we learned that vegetables must be seasoned with salt and pepper well and treated like everything else; not just drained and served. You want to extract the very best from your ingredients and it's amazing what a little butter, garlic and salt can do.

YOU WILL NEED:
1 large broccoli head, broken into florets
4 tbsp (60 ml) butter
2 garlic cloves, peeled and chopped

1 Drop the broccoli into a pan of salted boiling water. Cook for 5 to 8 minutes until the broccoli are soft when pricked with a knife. (Leave the lid off or they will lose their beautiful color.)

2 Drain the broccoli and tip them back into the saucepan.

3 Add the butter and garlic, then season well with salt and pepper.

4 Transfer to a serving dish and serve immediately.

Optional Extras: Replace the butter with olive oil if you want a lighter taste. A few pine nuts are amazing scattered on the top of the broccoli.

Serving Suggestions: These can be served with anything from a delicious roast (see pages 110–111) to a shepherd's pie (see pages 100–101) or fish pie (see pages 102–103). Or you could just eat them on their own—still amazing.

Leftovers: Green vegetables aren't the best when reheated as they turn quite soggy. However, cold broccoli are delicious in a salad or with some cold fish.

GOOEY LEEK GRATIN
SERVES 6

YOU WILL NEED:
4 tbsp (60 ml) butter
6 leeks, sliced
1 1/4 cups (300 ml) heavy cream
9 oz (250 g) cheddar cheese, grated

Every time I cooked a roast at university, this dish was always requested. I adore leeks anyway; I think they are versatile. When combined with cream and cheese and browned off in the oven, they are sensational.

Preheat the oven to 350°F (180°C).

1 Melt the butter in a skillet, then add the leeks and fry over medium heat.

2 The leeks will start to separate and shrivel up a little. Cook for 4 minutes until soft and then transfer to a deep ovenproof dish. I use one 8 inches (20 cm) in diameter.

3 Pour over the cream and sprinkle with the cheese.

4 Place in the oven for 15 minutes until the cheese is melted, golden and sensational.

Optional Extras: Use Gruyère cheese for gorgeous added decadence. It's not as reasonable as cheddar but is heaven when melted.

Serving Suggestions: A bit like cauliflower cheese, this is amazing on its own; however, I adore it with roast chicken (see pages 110–111).

Leftovers: Cover the cooked dish and keep in the refrigerator for up to 2 days. To reheat, place it in the oven at 250°F (130°C) for 15 minutes until hot.

BEEF STEW SERVES 6

What's not to love about a good hearty beef stew with some amazing mashed potatoes and red wine? It's also very reasonable to make, as you need to use stew beef, which is cheap.

Preheat the oven to 325°F (170°C).

1 Find a large ovenproof casserole dish. If you don't have one, use a large saucepan and just cook it on the stove rather than in the oven. Crumble the stock cubes into the boiling water. Stir and set aside.

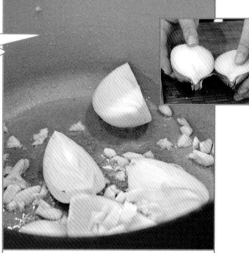

2 Heat the oil in the pan. Fry the onion and garlic for 3 to 4 minutes over medium heat until soft.

3 Toss the beef in the flour then add it to the pan for 2 to 3 minutes.

4 Add the carrots and leeks, stir well and season with salt and pepper.

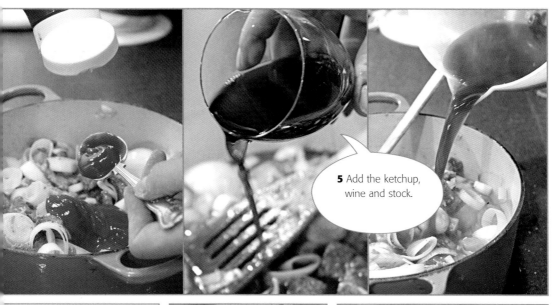

5 Add the ketchup, wine and stock.

6 Mix well and throw in the sprigs of rosemary.

7 Cover with a lid and put in the oven for 2½ to 3 hours. Or, leave on the stove on low heat for the same amount of time, stirring occasionally.

8 Check the stew after 2½ hours by cutting a piece of the meat in half. If it falls apart easily it's done. Also taste and check the seasoning. Serve hot on a mountain of mashed potato.

Optional Extras: Add some chopped herbs such as sage or rosemary when cooking the garlic and onion—that is so good. You could use the same amount of tomato paste if you don't want to use ketchup. Also pearl onions are amazing in stews, and instead of an onion you could use 6 pearl onions or even shallots peeled and chucked in with the garlic.
Serving Suggestions: Try this with some gorgeous garlic mashed potato (see page 83), and some red wine. So easy.
Leftovers: A cooked beef stew will keep in the refrigerator for 2 to 3 days. To reheat it, simply place it back on the stove, bring to a boil and serve piping hot. It's also lovely with boiled potatoes and a green salad.

CHICKEN, BACON AND MUSHROOM CASSEROLE SERVES 6

I have cooked this dish so many times—it's really reliable and so delicious. It was inspired by a recipe I was taught at the Ballymaloe Cookery School in Ireland and is perfect comfort food.

YOU WILL NEED:

- 4–5 tbsp (60–75 ml) olive oil
- 6 pearl onions or shallots, peeled
- 5 garlic cloves, peeled and crushed lightly
- 3 carrots, peeled and chopped
- 7 oz (200 g) baby white mushrooms
- 1¼ cups (200 g) diced bacon
- 6 chicken thighs
- 2 glasses of white wine
- 2 cups (475 ml) boiling water
- 2 chicken stock cubes
- 4–6 sprigs of thyme

Preheat the oven to 350°F (180°C).

1 Heat 2 tbsp (30 ml) of the oil in a large skillet and throw in the onions and garlic.

2 Cook on medium heat for 2 to 3 minutes, then transfer to a large casserole dish or an ovenproof saucepan.

3 Put the skillet back on the heat and add the carrots. Cook them for 2 minutes until slightly colored, then add to the casserole.

4 Repeat this process with the mushrooms and then the bacon. If the skillet gets dry, add some more olive oil.

5 Add 2 more tbsp (30 ml) of oil to the skillet and add the chicken thighs. Cook for 2 minutes on each side, just give them a golden color. Transfer to the casserole.

6 Return the skillet to the heat and heat half the white wine. Be careful as it might spit. Then pour it into the casserole; this is known as deglazing.

7 Tip the rest of the wine straight into the casserole.

If the sauce is too liquid, transfer 1³/₄ cups (400 ml) into a saucepan and add 4 tbsp (60 ml) butter and ⅓ cup (50 g) flour to thicken it. Then tip it back into the casserole.

8 Mix the boiling water with the stock cubes. Tip into the casserole with the thyme. Season well and cook in the oven for 45 minutes.

9 Check the chicken is cooked by cutting into the thickest part of the leg or breast. The meat should be white with no obvious signs of pink.

10 Serve now or keep it warm in the oven at 250°F (130°C) for 20 minutes.

Optional Extras: If you wanted to make this a vegetarian casserole, just remove the chicken and bacon and add some red onions, leeks, sugar snap peas and potatoes. Just cook them in the skillet like you do all other ingredients and transfer to the casserole.

Serving Suggestions: For me there is only one way to eat this—with gorgeous creamy mashed potatoes (see page 82) and a green salad.

Leftovers: A cooked casserole will keep in the refrigerator for 3 days. To reheat, simply place it back on the stove, bring to a boil and serve piping hot.

LOTTIE'S CHICKEN AND COCONUT CURRY

SERVES 4–6

My friend Lottie invited quite a few of us around one night and stunned us all with this absolute winner. A recipe for success, it was not only utterly delicious, but it also fueled us with energy to party into the early hours.

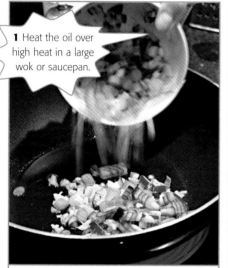

1 Heat the oil over high heat in a large wok or saucepan.

2 Add the garlic, scallions, red onion and ginger, turn the heat down to medium and fry for 2 minutes.

3 Raise the heat a bit to medium-high, stir in the curry paste and fry for 1 minute.

4 Reduce the heat to medium and add the chicken breasts and red bell pepper, followed by the coconut milk.

5 Bring this to a boil by raising the heat to high. Then reduce the heat to medium again to maintain a steady simmer. Simmer for 7 to 10 minutes, then check your chicken is cooked by cutting open one of the slices to make sure that it's all white with no sign of pink flesh.

6 Taste, and if it's too intensely coconutty for your liking, add the chicken stock. It's totally up to you.

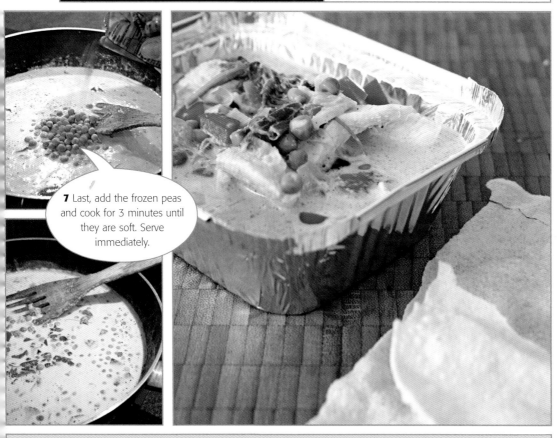

7 Last, add the frozen peas and cook for 3 minutes until they are soft. Serve immediately.

Optional Extras: Well, you could add some potatoes, or sweet potatoes. Butternut squash would be delicious too.

Leftovers: This will keep in the refrigerator for up to 2 days. Reheat it slowly in a pan until piping hot, if it seems too dry add ¼ cup (50 ml) chicken stock. Try serving it with noodles this time (see page 68).

Serving Suggestions: Serve sprinkled with cilantro or parsley alongside some basmati rice and maybe some papadums, if you wish.

FRAGRANT VEGETABLE CURRY

SERVES 4

Even though I am not a vegetarian, I'm a big fan of vegetable curries. After some playing around with ingredients, I have decided that sweet potatoes are the key to success for this recipe.

YOU WILL NEED:
1 eggplant, chopped into cubes
2 carrots, peeled and sliced
5½ oz (140 g) green beans
2 sweet potatoes, peeled and chopped into cubes
1¾ cups (400 ml) water
2 tbsp (30 ml) vegetable oil
1 red onion, peeled and chopped roughly
3 garlic cloves, peeled, finely chopped and crushed
1 green chili, sliced
2 tbsp (30 ml) curry paste
2 tbsp (30 ml) coconut milk
2 tbsp (30 ml) plain yogurt
3 tomatoes, quartered
handful of chopped cilantro leaves

1 Put the eggplant, carrots, green beans and sweet potatoes in a large saucepan, add the water and bring to a boil.

4 Add the curry paste. Stir well and cook for 2 minutes.

2 Cover and cook for 5 to 8 minutes over medium heat until the vegetables are tender. There won't be enough water to cover all the vegetables but that's fine. This will steam them more than boil them.

3 Meanwhile, heat the oil in a large wok, then add the onion, garlic and chili and stir-fry on medium heat until soft.

6 Spoon in the coconut milk. Mix well and season with salt and pepper.

5 Add your cooked vegetables, including the cooking water.

7 Add the yogurt and tomatoes.

8 Cook for another 2 to 3 minutes and then throw in the cilantro leaves at the end.

Optional Extras: ½ tsp (2 ml) of cumin seeds would be great here. Feel free to replace the vegetables with others that you like better. You could also cook the vegetables in vegetable stock instead of water for more flavor.

Serving Suggestions: Serve with some delicious Thai Fragrant Rice (see page 125).

Leftovers: Keep covered in the refrigerator and eat the following day, perhaps with noodles for a change. To reheat, place in a wok or saucepan and cook for about 5 minutes until piping hot.

HOW TO COOK RICE
SERVES 1

YOU WILL NEED:

generous ⅓ cup (75 g) basmati rice or long-grain rice

This is an easy way to cook rice that will guarantee delicious results—light and fluffy grains that are perfectly cooked every time. Rice is one of those versatile and cheap ingredients, like pasta, which can be kept in your pantry and will always come in handy as an accompaniment. Yet it can also be a delicious meal in its own right, with just a few extra bits thrown in. I most often use basmati rice whenever I'm cooking rice. In Hindi it means "Queen of fragrance" and is delicious with curries. I also adore it just with some butter and cilantro. Long-grain rice is cooked and prepared in the same way.

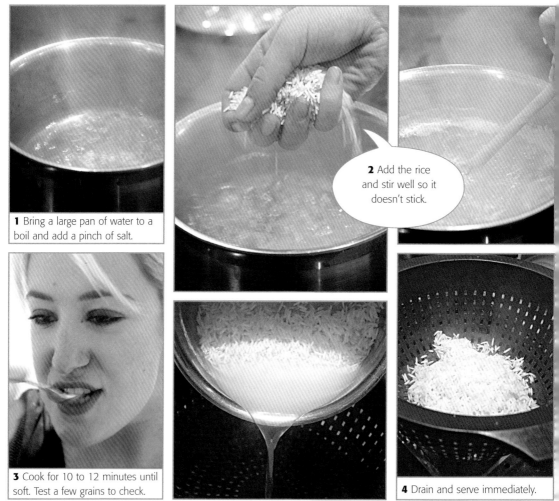

1 Bring a large pan of water to a boil and add a pinch of salt.

2 Add the rice and stir well so it doesn't stick.

3 Cook for 10 to 12 minutes until soft. Test a few grains to check.

4 Drain and serve immediately.

BUTTERED BASMATI WITH CILANTRO SERVES 4

Never associate simplicity with lack of taste or flavor. I could eat bowls of rice cooked like this. Just two extra ingredients add so much flavor.

YOU WILL NEED:

1³/₄ cups (350 g) basmati rice

scant ¹/₂ cup (100 g) butter

4 tbsp (60 ml) finely chopped cilantro leaves

Optional Extras: If you're not a fan of cilantro which I know many aren't, then use Italian parsley instead.
Serving Suggestions: Serve with a delicious curry or even a casserole.
Leftovers: Make sure you cool the rice properly before storing it in the fridge for 3 to 5 days.

1 Cook the rice as shown opposite.

2 Add in the butter, mix well and season with salt and pepper.

3 Scatter with the cilantro and mix well.

THAI FRAGRANT RICE SERVES 4

I love this rice, it's sensual and such good food. Similar to basmati, it is slightly stickier. It would be delicious with curry, or you could just serve it with some vegetables and soy sauce for a delicious dish in its own right.

YOU WILL NEED:

4 cups (1 liter) boiling water

1³/₄ cups (350 g) jasmine rice

juice of ¹/₂ lime

Serving Suggestions: Serve with Asian dishes, such as Shrimp and Coconut Stir-Fry (see page 70).

1 Boil the water in a large pan and add the rice. Stir well so the grains do not stick.

2 Cook for 10 minutes until the rice is soft, then drain it through a colander.

3 Tip the rice into a serving bowl and squeeze the lime juice over it.

AFRICAN BROWN RICE SERVES 4

I have been lucky to visit Portugal quite often. They cook so beautifully and it's interesting learning about and tasting foreign food. There's always something I pick up that I then cook back at home. This is a very simple rice dish from a superb restaurant called Dos Passos in the Algarve. I spent a morning in their kitchen and was taught how they make it.

1 Cook the rice as on page 124, but only boil it for 4 to 5 minutes as you want the rice still to have a good bit of bite.

2 Drain the rice, run it under cold water for 2 minutes and set aside.

3 Heat the oil in a large saucepan and add the onion and garlic. Cook on medium-low heat for 15 minutes until they are very soft.

4 Raise the heat and add the bacon. After a minute reduce the heat back to medium-low and cook for 10 minutes.

5 Tip in the rice and stir well, mixing everything together. Then add the soy sauce and stir well. The rice will turn light brown.

6 Cook on medium heat for 15 minutes, as you want the saltiness of the soy to evaporate.

7 At the end, throw in the currants or raisins and serve.

Optional Extras: I wouldn't add anything extra here, as this is how the Portuguese do it and it's the best.
Serving Suggestions: Serve with something simple like some broiled chicken or fish. It's very rich, so you wouldn't want it with anything too strong.
Leftovers: It's not best reheated, so keep eating.

SPECIAL FRIED RICE

SERVES 4

This is great for using up and emptying the refrigerator of random bits that you're not sure where or how to use. My mom calls it a "whip around the refrigerator" night when she cooks this.

YOU WILL NEED:

- 1½ cups (300 g) long-grain or basmati rice
- 2 tbsp (30 ml) olive oil
- 1 cup (200 g) diced bacon
- 1 onion, chopped
- 2 garlic cloves, peeled, finely chopped and crushed
- 7 oz (200 g) cooked chicken, beef or lamb leftovers
- 1¾ cups (200 g) frozen peas

1 Cook the rice as shown on page 124.

4 Throw in the chicken, beef or lamb.

2 Heat the oil in a skillet and add the bacon, onion and garlic. Fry until the bacon is golden.

3 Drain the rice and throw it in the pan with the onion and bacon, mixing well. Season with salt and pepper.

6 Mix everything together and serve—it's as easy as that.

5 Add the peas and cook for another 4 to 5 minutes, stirring.

Optional Extras: Add some chopped parsley, for a bit more green. A nice sliced red chili would be delicious and would also give it a real kick. Adding 1 tbsp (15 ml) of sweet chili sauce along with the peas would be gorgeous too.
Serving Suggestions: Amazing on its own with a salad. Great as well with some roasted chicken or stir-fried vegetables.
Leftovers: It's not the best reheated, so eat up!

8

HOUSE PARTIES

House parties are a brilliant opportunity to get everyone together for a big feast and the ultimate party. At university, everyone jumps at the invite to a house party, but make sure that they bring some booze and food if you like.

The recipes in this chapter are for eight or more, although you could double or even triple the quantities if needed. It's great to have a huge bowl of curry and just watch everyone dig in. Also I'm a major fan of barbecues whatever the season; I often do one around Halloween, when everyone can go outside in the backyard (providing it's not raining) to enjoy hot sausages and mulled wine. The perfect winter evening!

CHILI CON CARNE
SERVES 8

A hot and warming Chili Con Carne is quite simply an ultimate favorite and perfect for a house party when feeding the masses. I love a good bit of spice, so chilies and red pepper flakes are brilliant in this. Place it on the table when you're done and just watch the fight as everyone rushes over. Great with a cold beer or some red wine.

YOU WILL NEED:

- 4 tbsp (60 ml) olive oil
- 2 red onions, chopped finely
- 4 garlic cloves, chopped finely
- 2 red chilies, seeded and chopped finely
- 2 tsp (10 ml) red pepper flakes
- 3 lb (1.5 kg) lean ground beef
- 3 x 14 oz (400 g) cans chopped tomatoes
- 2 glasses of red wine (optional)
- 1 tbsp (15 ml) Worcestershire sauce
- 1 tsp (5 ml) Tabasco sauce
- 1½ lb (800 g) red kidney beans
- ⅔ cup (150 ml) sour cream

Finely chop the onions, garlic and chilies.

2 Add the red pepper flakes. Cook gently for 3 to 4 minutes

You should be hit with the smells of the garlic and spice—all great.

1 Heat the olive oil in a skillet on medium heat. Add the red onions, garlic and fresh chilies.

3 Turn the heat right up and add the ground beef. Season well and cook until brown.

4 Reduce the heat to medium and add the tomatoes, red wine, Worcestershire sauce and Tabasco sauce. Stir well and then add the kidney beans.

6 Serve hot with a dollop of sour cream.

5 Simmer for as long as time allows. I like this to simmer for at least an hour, so all the flavors really intensify. Taste it after an hour and adjust the seasoning accordingly.

Need a bigger bowl.

I can feed myself, you know.

Optional Extras: Don't add the Tabasco sauce if you don't like it too hot, but it does give it a real kick. Chopped parsley or cilantro would be great at the end, sprinkled over.

Serving Suggestions: I like this with rice and some sour cream, Guacamole (see page 78) and maybe a side salad. It's so easy to do for large numbers.

Leftovers: Never throw away any leftover chili; it's excellent the next day, as it just seems to get better and better. It's great reheated slowly in a saucepan until hot and then served in a baked potato with grated cheese. Recovery food.

MY ULTIMATE THAI GREEN CURRY

SERVES 6–8

I have requests for this when my friends are hungover or, weirdly, when they have a cold. Fragrant Thai food with a little spice really clears blocked noses, and is just so comforting. This is also perfect food to do when you have lots of people around as, like chili, you can place it on the table with some rice and just let everyone dig in.

YOU WILL NEED:

4 tbsp (60 ml) vegetable oil
4 garlic cloves, peeled and chopped finely
¾-inch (2 cm) piece of ginger, peeled and chopped finely
4 scallions, sliced
3 lemongrass stalks, peeled and chopped finely
2 green chilies, seeded and chopped finely
grated zest and juice of 6 limes
4 tbsp (60 ml) Thai green curry paste
2¼ lb (1 kg) chicken breasts or pieces, sliced
5 cups (1.2 liters) coconut milk (3 x 14 oz/400 ml cans)
1 chicken stock cube
¾ cup (175 ml) boiling water
1¼ lb (600 g) green beans, trimmed
2 handfuls torn cilantro

1 Heat the oil in a skillet over medium heat. Add the garlic, ginger, scallions, lemongrass and chilies. Stir-fry for 3 to 4 minutes until they are soft.

2 Raise the heat and add the lime zest and juice.

3 Stir in the curry paste.

4 Stir-fry for 3 minutes then add the chicken.

6 Mix the stock cube into the boiling water. Pour into the pan.

7 Simmer for 5 minutes until the chicken is cooked.

5 Stir the chicken around well, then add the coconut milk immediately.

8 Then add in the green beans and cook for another 5 minutes.

Check the chicken is cooked by cutting open a slice to make sure there is no sign of pink flesh.

9 Scatter with cilantro and serve.

Optional Extras: Green bell peppers would work very well instead of the green beans, and if you want it not to be so green you could use red chilies instead of green.

Serving Suggestions: This is great if you're feeding a crowd. Serve it with some boiled rice, or even just some papadums. If you're eating this in a smaller group, noodles would be amazing.

Leftovers: Put any leftovers in an airtight container and keep for up to 2 days in the refrigerator or for up to 3 months in the freezer. To reheat, defrost thoroughly and reheat gently in a saucepan until piping hot.

VODKA WATERMELON

SERVES 8 OR MORE

YOU WILL NEED:

1 watermelon

generous ¼ cup (60 ml) vodka

This is such fun, and perfect for a house party. Watermelon is at its best and is also most available during the summer.

2 Knife out the flesh at the top of the incision. Use a spoon to dig a hole as far down to the center as you can.

1 Take the watermelon and using a knife carefully cut a hole about 2 inches (5 cm) wide.

3 Pour the vodka into the hole, put the watermelon "lid" back on and leave for an hour.

Watch out, it's stronger than you think …

5 Then you can cut it open and eat all the melon, which will have soaked up all the remaining vodka.

4 When your friends come around, grab a lot of straws and sip up the melon-y vodka.

DELICIOUS COSMOPOLITAN COCKTAIL SERVES 1

YOU WILL NEED:

¼ cup (60 ml) vodka

2 tbsp (30 ml) cranberry juice

juice of 1 lime

This is a great cocktail and perfect with the lime and chili shrimp kebabs (see page 138). It has a little lime juice in it, which enhances the lime in the shrimp. It's also pink, punchy and fun.

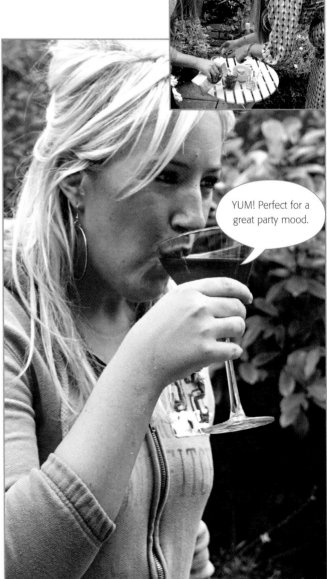

YUM! Perfect for a great party mood.

1 Pour the vodka into a large glass and add the cranberry and lime juices.

BARBECUE SELECTION

At university, the start of summer is obviously a fun time; however, it means one thing: EXAMS. Everyone is in need of a good dinner and to destress after days of endless studying. So why not have a small house party and do a barbecue? Chicken thighs, kebabs and sausages are all great for lifting the mood, especially with a cheeky cocktail to wash it all down. Don't feel you have to limit barbecues to the summer. I always do one on Halloween, then have tons of friends around along with some mulled wine and sausages in the backyard. Whatever the occasion, these are great for a cheap, relaxed party night.

SAUSAGES

A barbecue staple, and so, so delicious with a bit of ketchup. Don't save them just for summer, they're great in winter too, and great for a Halloween party. Cocktail franks would be scrumptious here too.

YOU WILL NEED:

16 sausages
4 tbsp (60 ml) honey
2 tbsp (30 ml) sesame seeds
(optional)

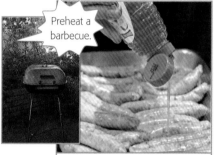

Preheat a barbecue.

1 Place the sausages in a dish and pour over the honey. Mix well.

Turn them over halfway through.

2 Place the sausages on the barbecue and cook over the hot coals for 10 minutes until golden brown.

3 Put the cooked sausages in a bowl and sprinkle with the sesame seeds, if you're using them. If they don't stick very well, drizzle in another 1 tbsp (15 ml) of honey.

Dig in.

Optional Extras: Sausages are amazing on their own, so if you don't want to add the honey or sesame seeds then just cook them without. I just love the stickiness that comes from the honey. Wrap a slice of bacon around each sausage for an extra meat fest.
Serving Suggestions: Dip in lots of ketchup and mustard.
Leftovers: These are great eaten cold, and can be kept in the refrigerator, covered, for 2 days. To reheat, place in a pan and cook for 5 minutes until hot. Have a sausage sandwich to nurse away the hangover after your party.

HONEY AND MUSTARD CHICKEN SERVES 10

YOU WILL NEED:
10 chicken thighs, drumsticks or wings
3 tbsp (45 ml) runny honey
3 tbsp (45 ml) mustard

Any barbecue would be incomplete without barbecued chicken. This marinade gives the meat a delicious sweet-savory edge that tastes amazing with the smoky flavors from the barbecue.

3 Use your hands to rub the mixture all over the chicken.

1 Place all the chicken pieces in a large dish.

2 Smother with honey and mustard.

If you're making this in advance, which is always great whenever you marinate something, put it in the refrigerator for 30 minutes. Or even better, make it in the morning and keep it in the refrigerator all day so the flavors of the honey and mustard have more time to soak into the meat.

4 When your barbecue is hot, put the chicken on it, turning every 3 minutes. Cook for about 10 minutes until they are crispy, golden brown and cooked through. To check that they are thoroughly cooked, cut one open— there should be no sign of pink flesh, just white chicken meat.

Optional Extras: To spice up the marinade a little, add some hot chili sauce, or even a finely chopped red or green chili. Herbs such as rosemary, chopped finely and rubbed onto the chicken, would also be delicious.
Serving Suggestion: Staple barbecue sauces of course: ketchup, mayonnaise, barbecue sauce. Serve along with other barbecue classics, such as sausages, burgers and salad.

LIME AND CHILI SHRIMP KEBABS

SERVES 10

YOU WILL NEED:

10 oz (300 g) cooked and peeled shrimp
juice of 3 limes
2 red chilies, seeded and chopped finely
2 tbsp (30 ml) soy sauce
20 wooden toothpicks or skewers

These are so pungent and a real tasty treat. Supermarkets do great deals on ready cooked and peeled shrimp and they are often quite an economical treat. As always with fish, if you are near to a fish supplier, pop in to check on the prices of some little cooked and peeled shrimp against the supermarkets.

Soak the toothpicks or skewers in water—this prevents them from burning on the barbecue.

This is great if left to marinate in the refrigerator for a few hours, but if you're short of time then 10 to 30 minutes is better than nothing.

1 Put the shrimp in a bowl; add the lime juice, chilies and soy sauce. Stir around well.

Don't forget that since the shrimp have already been cooked, you're not trying to cook them, just crisp them up and warm them through.

2 Thread the shrimp onto the presoaked toothpicks or skewers.

3 Spoon over any remaining juices at the bottom of your bowl and then place the kebabs on the barbecue for 5 minutes.

Serving Suggestions: So good dipped in some soy sauce or even some sweet chili sauce, or just squeeze some lime juice over them before serving and you're done.

BARBECUED BANANAS SERVES 10

If you're having a barbecue, this is a sensational and ridiculously simple dessert. Just place the whole bananas on the barbecue, slit them open and fill them with a variety of fillings. Delish …

YOU WILL NEED:

10 bananas

Filling options:

10 tbsp (150 ml) sugar

11 oz (300 g) milk or dark chocolate, broken into pieces

You don't want it red hot or the skin of the bananas will blister.

1 Place the whole bananas on a barbecue that has been used and therefore is just cooling down.

2 Turn them over after 5 minutes and the skin should be black. Don't panic, this is what you're looking for.

3 After another 5 minutes both sides should be black and the bananas might be bubbling a little through the skin. Remove them from the barbecue.

4 Slit the bananas open lengthwise and gently pull them open, leaving the skin intact.

5 Divide the chocolate between the bananas and sprinkle with the sugar.

Eat immediately. Amazing!

Optional Extras: This is one of those dishes that are very personal; everyone always seems to have their own favorite combinations. You could add marshmallows, 1 tbsp (15 ml) of cream per banana, or 1 tbsp (15 ml) of custard in each one—it's up to you.

Serving Suggestions: A scoop of ice cream would be amazing with these bananas. Hot and cold together—yum. Don't hang about though, eat the bananas while they're still warm.

Leftovers: It would be a worry if there were any left!

THE ULTIMATE HOT CHOCOLATE

SERVES 1

When I was at school I had a coffee shop that was my savior and I went there a few days a week after school for one of their epic hot chocolates. Marshmallows in hot chocolate—whoever came up with that is a hero!

YOU WILL NEED:

1 tbsp (15 ml) cocoa powder, plus extra to decorate

1¼ cups (300 ml) milk

4 tbsp (60 ml) heavy cream, whipped

small handful of marshmallows

1 Take a large mug and spoon in the cocoa powder.

2 Gently heat your milk in a pan.

3 When the milk is hot pour it into the mug with the cocoa powder, stirring all the time.

4 Whip the cream.

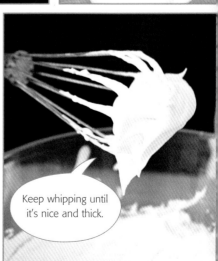

Keep whipping until it's nice and thick.

5 When it's thick and stiff spoon it on top of the chocolate drink.

6 Push in the marshmallows.

7 Dust with a bit of cocoa powder.

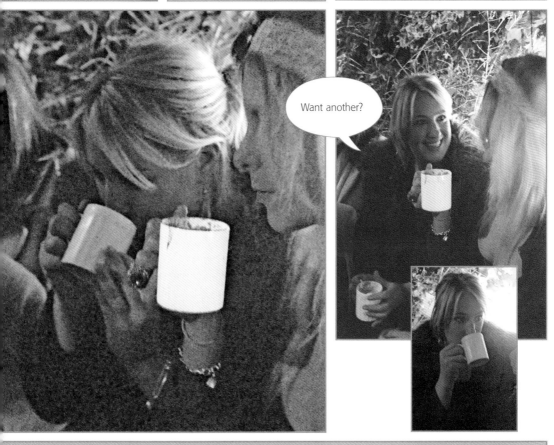

Want another?

Optional Extras: A tsp (5 ml) of whisky would be fantastic and give this a real kick.
Serving Suggestions: Drink on its own, or with some lovely chocolate to nibble on while you chill out and chat.

9

TIFF'S TREATS

If you've got a sweet tooth, this is the chapter for you—a selection of my much-loved home desserts. I've also added some irresistible sweet bites, such as chocolate brownies and cute cupcakes that are perfect to grab and go. Cakes have a reputation for being a bit tricky, but all these recipes are really easy, so you might feel a bit of a fraud when your friends tell you how impressed they are. Say nothing and just accept the compliments! There's something in here for everyone: a gorgeous birthday cake that would be even better than an actual present; a comforting hot apple crumble; and a banana bread that's ideal for the occasional coffee break, or in my case not so occasional.

BRILLIANT CHOCOLATE BROWNIES

MAKES 20 MEDIUM SIZE BROWNIES

YOU WILL NEED:

1 cup (225 g) butter, plus
2 tbsp (30 ml) for greasing
10 oz (275 g) dark or milk
chocolate, broken into pieces
4 medium eggs
1⅓ cups (275 g) soft brown suga
1½ cups (200 g) all-purpose flou
½ tsp (2 ml) baking powder

The secret here is the brown sugar, which makes the brownies go ever so gooey and soft. A brownie should have a crispy top and then a gorgeous squidgy center. These hit the spot perfectly.

Preheat the oven to 350°F (180°C).

1 Grease a 12 inch by 8 inch (30 cm by 20 cm) baking pan with butter. Line it with waxed paper.

2 Melt the chocolate and butter in a saucepan until they make a smooth mixture. Set aside to cool for a few minutes.

3 Beat the eggs in a bowl and mix in the brown sugar.

4 Add the chocolate mixture and stir well.

5 Gently add the flour and baking powder, stirring until evenly mixed.

6 Pour the batter into the lined pan and bake in the hot oven for 25 minutes.

7 Remove from the oven. It should have a wonderful crisp top yet the brown sugar will have made it sensationally gooey in the middle.

8 Cut into squares (you choose the size) and serve.

Optional Extras: I'm not a great fan of nutty brownies, but if you like them, feel free to add a handful of walnuts when you add the flour. You could of course use superfine sugar instead of soft brown sugar.

Serving Suggestions: Serve as a delicious afternoon treat, or even as a dessert with some vanilla ice cream. Mini brownies are great if you've got lots of friends coming over.

Leftovers: These will keep for 3 days in an airtight container.

CHOCOLATE MOUSSE

SERVES 6–8

I make this mousse with egg white rather than cream, as it's healthier and also gives it an incredibly light and fluffy texture. Pour it into wine glasses, put them in the refrigerator to set and then top with some fresh fruit. Seriously easy, yet surprisingly impressive.

YOU WILL NEED:

12 oz (350 g) milk chocolate, broken into chunks

4 medium eggs

⅔ cup (150 g) butter

scant ½ cup (75 g) superfine sugar

1⅓ cups (150 g) blueberries

1 Melt the chocolate by putting it in a heatproof bowl over a pan of simmering water. Stir as it melts; this should take 3 to 4 minutes.

2 The bowl should fit snugly, but it shouldn't touch the water. Let the melted chocolate cool for 5 minutes.

3 Meanwhile, take 2 bowls and separate the eggs.

To do this, crack each egg open and allow the white to fall out while you keep the yolk in the shell. Tip the yolk gently between each shell half and let the rest of the egg white drop into the bowl. Tip the yolk into the second bowl. Repeat this process with the remaining eggs.

4 Beat the egg yolks with the melted chocolate. Then stir in the butter and sugar.

The whites should have stiff peaks.

Do this gently or else all the air will be beaten out of your egg whites and you'll be left with a flat mousse.

5 Whisk the egg whites in a large scrupulously-clean bowl for 3 to 5 minutes. An electric whisk would take about 2 minutes.

6 Gently fold the egg whites into the chocolate mixture.

7 Divide the mixture into bowls or glasses. Then let set in the refrigerator for 1 to 2 hours.

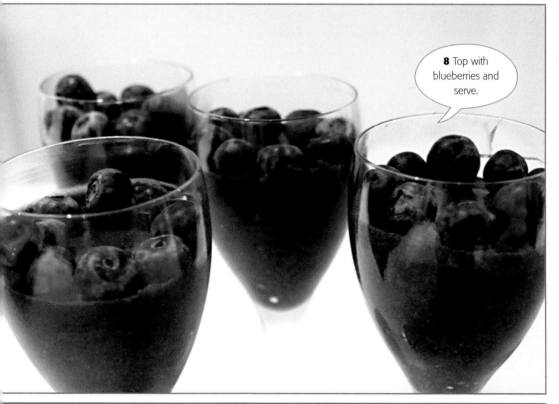

8 Top with blueberries and serve.

Optional Extras: You could whisk some passion fruit into the mousse. This works a treat with white chocolate mousse. Use whatever type of chocolate you like. I love milk, but semisweet chocolate is very popular as is white chocolate.
Serving Suggestions: Try strawberries or raspberries instead of blueberries.
Leftovers: The set mousse will keep in the refrigerator for 2 to 3 days. Always eat chilled.

APPLE CRUMBLE

SERVES 4–6

My grandmother makes a sensational apple crumble so I've stolen all her ideas. It's such a simple dessert and there are never any leftovers.

YOU WILL NEED:

5 large baking apples, peeled, cored and quartered
1¼ cups (300 ml) water
1 tsp (5 ml) lemon juice
2 tbsp (30 ml) granulated sugar

Crumble Topping:
2 cups (275 g) all-purpose flour
1 cup (175 g) granulated sugar
generous ¾ cup (200 g) butter, roughly cubed

Preheat the oven to 350°F (180°C).

1 Put the apples in a pan with the water, lemon juice and sugar. Cover with a lid and cook on medium heat for 15 minutes until soft. Taste and if they are a little sharp add a bit more sugar. If they're too sweet add another squeeze of lemon juice.

It will transform into a golden crumble, rather like lumpy sand.

2 Meanwhile, prepare the crumble topping.

3 Mix the flour and sugar together in a large bowl. Add the butter and use your hands to rub it into the flour. Be patient, the crumble will come together eventually.

4 Spread the apples across the bottom of an ovenproof dish (I use one 11 inches by 6.5 inches/30 cm by 17 cm), then sprinkle the crumble over the top.

5 Bake for 30 to 40 minutes until golden brown.

Optional Extras: You could add some raisins, blackberries, raspberries, nutmeg or even vanilla extract to the saucepan of apples. You could also swap the granulated sugar for brown sugar in the crumble mixture.
Serving Suggestions: Serve with a good dollop of vanilla ice cream.
Leftovers: If you have any leftovers then your friends are crazy. Keep in the refrigerator for up to 3 days and reheat in the oven for 10 minutes on 300°F (150°C).

BANANA BREAD

SERVES 6

This cake is perfect coffee break material when you've got lots of work. Reward yourself with a slice of banana bread and a cup of coffee.

YOU WILL NEED:

⅓ cup (75 g) butter
1 cup (175 g) superfine sugar
1 lb (450 g) bananas, peeled
2 medium eggs
scant 1½ cups (200 g) self-rising flour
¼ tsp (1 ml) baking soda
½ tsp (2 ml) salt

Preheat the oven to 350°F (180°C).

1 Grease a 2-lb (900 g) loaf pan with butter, then line it with a sheet of waxed paper.

2 In a bowl, beat together the butter and sugar. Chop the bananas and mash them into the mixture. Add the eggs and combine well.

3 Mix the flour, baking soda and salt together in a bowl.

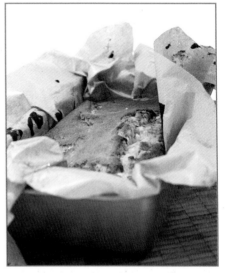

4 Sift the flour mixture into the banana and butter mixture and mix well until evenly combined.

5 Pour into the loaf pan and put it in the oven for 25 minutes until risen and golden brown.

Optional Extras: Walnuts are delicious. Add them at the same time as the bananas, but make sure no one eating it suffers from a nut allergy.
Serving Suggestions: Eat warm, perhaps spread with a little bit of butter.
Leftovers: This will keep in an airtight container for 3 days.

CUTE CUPCAKES MAKES ABOUT 20

Cupcakes have become very trendy and are everywhere—there are even stores dedicated entirely to cupcakes. They're perfect when you have lots of friends around and they're really easy to whip up.

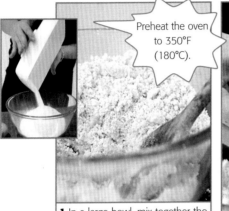

Preheat the oven to 350°F (180°C).

1 In a large bowl, mix together the flour, superfine sugar and butter until evenly combined.

2 Add the eggs and mix well.

The batter should be light and fluffy.

4 Bake in the oven for 15 to 20 minutes until golden. To check whether they're cooked, insert a skewer into a cake—if it comes out clean it's cooked, if not give it another 5 minutes. Remove from the oven to cool.

3 Put the cupcake cases on a cookie sheet and spoon 1 tbsp (15 ml) into each one.

I love adding food colorings to the frosting, as it's fun to have different colored cupcakes. So add any color you want.

5 Meanwhile, make the butter frosting. Mix the confectioners' sugar with the butter. It's very sweet, so you could do half butter and half cream cheese if you prefer.

6 Spread the frosting over the cupcakes.

7 Decorate with mini marshmallows or silver balls … It's up to you.

Optional Extras: You could add 1 tsp (5 ml) of vanilla extract to the cake batter.

Serving Suggestions: I love the cakes with different toppings. Get creative!

Leftovers: Unfrosted cakes will keep for 3 to 4 days in an airtight container. If they are frosted they need to go into the refrigerator.

OMA'S UPSIDE DOWN PINEAPPLE CAKE SERVES 6

Oma, my grandmother, is making a huge feature in this book, but her recipes are totally extraordinary. This is easy peasy, and canned pineapples are really cheap and readily available. This would be perfect after a student Sunday lunch or just after a weekday dinner.

YOU WILL NEED:
- ⅔ cup (150 g) butter
- ¾ cup (150 g) superfine sugar
- 1 tbsp (15 ml) corn syrup or honey (optional)
- 2x 7½ oz (220 g) cans pineapple slices (not chunks)
- 2 oz (50 g) candied cherries
- ¾ cup (110 g) self-rising flour
- 2 medium eggs, beaten

> Preheat the oven to 325°F (170°C).

1 Find a baking pan about 9 inches (23 cm) across and 1½ inches (4 cm) deep. Grease the pan with 2 tbsp (25 ml) of the butter.

2 Sprinkle in ⅛ cup (25 g) of the superfine sugar.

3 Drizzle in the corn syrup or honey. This is just delicious, but don't panic if you don't have any, it's fine to leave it out.

4 Arrange the pineapple rings in the dish. Don't throw away the pineapple juice as you may need it later. Fill any holes with bits of pineapple. Put the candied cherries inside the pineapple rings.

5 In a separate bowl, cream together the remaining butter and superfine sugar.

6 Tip in the self-rising flour and make a well for the eggs, then beat well.

7 The batter should have a good spreading consistency. If it seems too dry, however, add 1–2 tbsp (15–30 ml) of the pineapple juice.

8 Spread the batter evenly over the pineapples and bake for 20 minutes.

9 Remove the pan from the oven and insert a skewer into the sponge. If your skewer comes out clean, then the dessert is ready, if not, put it back in the oven for another 5 to 10 minutes before testing again. When ready, the sponge should be firm and golden. Let it cool for 5 to 10 minutes.

10 Remove the sides of the pan, put a plate upside down over the sponge and flip your dessert onto the plate. The pineapples will be on top and the sponge on the bottom.

Now dig in.

Leftovers: The cake will keep in an airtight container, such as a cookie tin, for 3 to 4 days.

Serving Suggestions: Delicious with ice cream. If you don't want to use pineapples, you could use pears or plums. You could also add 2 tbsp (30 ml) of cocoa powder to the batter to make a chocolate sponge—this is delicious with pears. You can also cook the dessert in the morning, put it in the refrigerator and then put it back in the oven for 5 to 10 minutes at 300°F (150°C) just before you want to serve it.

BIRTHDAY CAKE SERVES 6

Friends often ask me how to make a simple sponge birthday cake. This is a great recipe and very swift to whip up.

YOU WILL NEED:

1 cup (225 g) butter, plus extra for greasing

1⅛ cups (225 g) superfine sugar

3 large eggs, beaten

1⅔ cups (225 g) self-rising flour

Frosting:

⅔ cup (150 g) butter

1¾ cups (200 g) confectioners' sugar, plus 2 tbsp (30 ml)

2 tbsp (30 ml) strawberry or raspberry jam

Preheat the oven to 350°F (180°C).

1 Beat the butter and sugar together in a large bowl. Then add the eggs and mix well.

The batter will get tougher to mix as you add more flour, but persevere as it will eventually become smooth and creamy.

2 Slowly add the flour and keep mixing.

3 Grease a pair of 8½ inch (22 cm) cake pans with butter. Divide the batter between them.

This is the best bit.

4 Bake in the oven for 20 minutes until golden brown.

Check they are cooked by inserting a skewer. It's ready if it comes out clean.

5 Remove from the oven, set aside for 5 minutes then turn out onto a board or plate.

6 Make the frosting by beating the butter until smooth and then mixing in the confectioners' sugar.

7 When the cakes are cool, spread the frosting over one of the sponges. Spread the other sponge with jam and sandwich the two together.

8 Sift the 2 tbsp (30 ml) confectioners' sugar over the top.

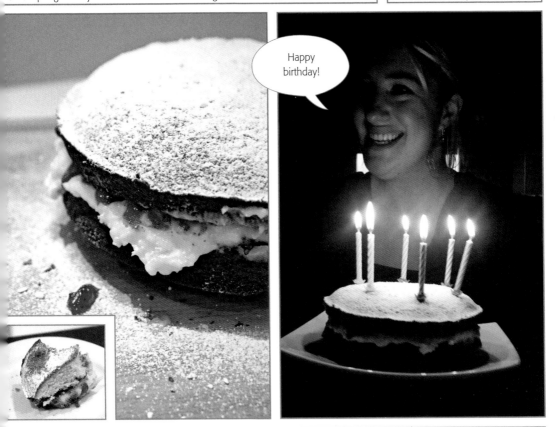

Happy birthday!

Optional Extras: You could decorate the cake with some fresh fruit, chocolate sprinkles or candies. There are so many bits you can buy for cake decorating, it just depends how far you want to go.

Serving Suggestions: I love decorating my cake with strawberries in the summer—it looks so pretty. In the winter, go for blackberries.

Leftovers: The cake will keep in an airtight container in the refrigerator for 1 to 2 days but not for much longer, as it will become soggy from the filling.

INDEX

A FIREFLY BOOK

ublished by Firefly Books Ltd. 2009

ext Copyright © 2009 Tiffany Goodall

ll photographs copyright © 2009
Quadrille Publishing Limited

esign and layout © 2009 Quadrille Publishing Limited

ixth Printing, 2014

ublisher Cataloging-in-Publication Data (U.S.)

oodall, Tiffany.
    The ultimate student cookbook: from chicken to chili /
ffany Goodall.
60] p. : col. photos. ; cm.
cludes index.
otes: Basic kitchen equipment -- Store cupboard ingredients
    Food hygiene.
ummary: A beginner's step-by-step guide to food
reparation and cooking.
BN-13: 978-1-55407-602-4 (pbk.)
. Cookery. I. Title.
41.5 dc22   TX714.G663   2010

Library and Archives Canada Cataloguing in Publication

Goodall, Tiffany
        The ultimate student cookbook : from chicken to
chili / Tiffany Goodall.
Includes index.
ISBN 978-1-55407-602-4
        1. Cookery. 2. Quick and easy cookery. I. Title.
TX652.G661 2009   641.5'12   C2009-904387-4

Published in the United States by
Firefly Books (U.S.) Inc.
P.O. Box 1338, Ellicott Station,
Buffalo, New York, 14205

Published in Canada by
Firefly Books Ltd.
50 Staples Avenue, Unit 1
Richmond Hill, Ontario L4B 0A7

Printed in China

First published by Quadrille Publishing Limited

EDITORIAL DIRECTOR Anne Furniss
ART DIRECTOR Helen Lewis
PROJECT EDITOR Katey Mackenzie
PHOTOGRAPHER Claire Peters
DESIGNER Katherine Case
PRODUCTION Vincent Smith, Aysun Hughes

ACKNOWLEDGMENTS

My love of food and cooking began at the famous and truly magical Ballymaloe Cookery School, Ireland. Darina Allen is one of the most knowledgable people I have ever met. Thank you for sharing your excitement about food; it is infectious. Rachel Allen, thank you for being a wonderful teacher too. My memories of my time there are so special.

Another big thank you goes to the amazing Martin Blunos for believing in me and all my ideas while we worked together for Marks and Spencer in deepest Derby. You generously introduced me to your, and now my agent Rosemary Melbourne. Rosemary, thank you for your solid belief that this would work, and for always being ahead of the game in every way. You have made so much possible for me—thank you. Without your introduction, I would never have met my incredible literary agents, Heather Holden Brown and Elly James. Thank you both for believing in the book and teaching me so much about the world of books and publishing. Elly, your constant support and our brainstorming sessions have been such a laugh.

A huge thank you to everyone at Quadrille. You have made me and my book feel very special and have worked so hard to make it unique. Anne Furniss, thank you for your faith in this project from day one. Helen Lewis, a big thank you for your creative ideas and for putting together an amazingly talented duo in the form of Katherine Case, a brilliant designer, and Claire Peters—I'm so excited to have been part of your first photography project. I know there will be more to come, the photos are beautiful. I am hugely grateful to my wonderful editor, Katey Mackenzie, who has worked tirelessly and has provided many giggles too.

There is a little fish and chip shop in Fulham which is where I learned all about hard work from aged 16 onward. "Fishers" has the best fish and chips in the world but it is also where I have a small family in the likes of Gary, Alan, Tom and Danny who I love.

Thank you to ALL of my wonderful friends. There are too many of you to thank but you have all been so supportive. Cress and Char for being there since Barbie days, Ingrid for coming to Chester and always being 100% supportive, and Bex for your pivotal role in Tiff's Tuesdays. A huge thank you to the famous five, you know who you are, for always wanting and encouraging Tiff's Tuesdays. Guy, you've been wonderful but especially at being a great guinea pig.

Betina, thank you for your support.

Oma, you are my inspiration and thank you for giving me so many cooking and recipe ideas and supplying some of your recipe secrets for the book.

My sisters, George and Kamillie; I think you are both budding young chefs. Mama if it hadn't been for you I would never have gone to Ballymaloe. You gave up your kitchen to me for filming, endless photos and an office. Thank you for *everything*, too much to mention here. Papa, you're always there, always supportive and always enthusiastic—thank you.